W9-DFY-818

DISCARDED
from the Nashville Public Library

# SALTY

# SALTY

Lessons on Eating, Drinking, and
Living from Revolutionary Women

ALISSA WILKINSON

BROADLEAF BOOKS
MINNEAPOLIS

SALTY

Lessons on Eating, Drinking, and
Living from Revolutionary Women

Copyright © 2022 Alissa Wilkinson. Printed by Broadleaf Books,
an imprint of 1517 Media. All rights reserved. Except for brief
quotations in critical articles or reviews, no part of this book
may be reproduced in any manner without prior written
permission from the publisher. Email copyright@1517.media
or write to Permissions, Broadleaf Books, PO Box 1209,
Minneapolis, MN 55440-1209.

Cover image: Plate & fork: shutterstock/Valumyan; Drink &
    cigarette: shutterstock/Natalia Hubbert; journal: shutterstock/
    Larysa Kaminska; parsley: shutterstock/Galyna Gryshchenko;
    ice: shutterstock/ Daria Ustiugova;
    Interior art by Jennifer Khatun
Cover design: Faceout Studios

Print ISBN: 978-1-5064-7355-0
eBook ISBN: 978-1-5064-7356-7


Printed in Canada

*For Tom, who is salt, light, and sweetness*

# CONTENTS

# INVITATION TO THE FEAST

This book is a dinner party, and you are invited.

Dinner parties are among life's greatest pretenses. Everybody has to eat dinner. When your host invites you, that's what structures the evening: the meal.

But really, a dinner party is an excuse to create and deepen friendships, to form alliances, to encounter new ideas, to stretch yourself. It's an invitation to risk something, to put yourself out there just a little, with the comforting universal activity of eating dinner as an excuse and a task to accomplish. A dinner party creates a universe.

This dinner party is not a very proper dinner party. We'll be using paper towels instead of cloth napkins, and you might have to drink wine from the wrong kind of glass. Some of the guests are probably going to arrive at the wrong time. There's a good chance at least one of the dishes won't match the others at all.

No matter. This is a dinner party for people with more than simple social niceties on their minds.

You may know some of the other guests. Others may be strangers. When you first arrive, please chat with them while you enjoy the appetizers—a salty, crisp martini, perhaps, and some soft, crumbly blue cheese with peppery crackers on the side. You can break the ice with chatter about the weather or your work, but there are plenty of other things to discuss: books, movies, ideas, travel. Even politics and religion aren't off the table, as long as you don't assume too much about other people's sympathies and proclivities. We're here to make a community, not just pass the evening.

When the food comes out, though, everyone's job is to dig in. Maybe you're eating a roast chicken rubbed with salt and pepper and placed on top of a bed of potatoes that have turned buttery and soft. Or a big pot of autumnal stew full of orange and red and brown vegetable chunks floating in a savory, tangy tomato broth, roughly torn pieces of bread and hunks of gouda on the side. Or a spicy shrimp salad, creamy and delicious, with a delightful crunch thanks to astringent bits of celery, served over leaves of lettuce. There may be pitchers of sparkling mineral water or tall bottles of dry white wine. When the entrée is over, perhaps you eat slices of pound cake with strawberries and crème fraîche, or a peach cobbler with vanilla ice cream, with small glasses of port or cups of mint tea. Whatever the case, this is not the time to hew to rules and portion control. It's a feast. As much as you're able, treat it accordingly.

The thing about dinner parties is that you never know who will be there. During pre-dinner chatter, you may realize that a couple of guests are opinionated, brash, a little intimidating. You might sit far away from them at dinner, but they're intriguing. When the pair walks out to the balcony for some air and a post-meal cigarette, you could gather up your courage and your cocktail and follow, wondering what they'll talk about.

And out in the cold air, delight might spread from your toes to your heart. These are women with strong opinions, but also generous ones. They aren't arguing just for argument's sake—they have a passion for truth and for the ongoing work of community. They call you over, asking you what you think, finding out about your story. When the host calls you back in for a nightcap, you sit near them, listening, learning, realizing that there's something revolutionary happening here.

Because, it turns out, the little world that's been created here at this dinner party is not just a place to eat dinner or make friends. It's not a place designed to make you admire someone's outfits or envy their real estate. It's a more dangerous space—a gathering where flinty iron strikes against iron, throwing sparks on your own mind. It's where what you thought you knew about the world gets prodded and pulled and stretched and even snapped.

So when it's all over, when you're pulling on coats and wrapping scarves around necks, if you've met someone at the table you'd like to talk to again, don't be shy. Ask them if you can get in touch and talk about the things that scared you, the causes you have in common, the work they do and how you can be part of it. The greatest pleasure for any host is when two strangers who met at the feast table become friends, fellow travelers, comrades in arms.

In the Brooklyn Museum, not far from my dinner table, is the great feminist artist Judy Chicago's most well-known work, *The Dinner Party*, which was first exhibited in 1979. Three tables are arranged like a triangle, with thirteen ornate place settings on each table. Each setting is designed and designated for a great woman in history, from the ancient poet Sappho to Saint Hildegard of Bingen to Mary Wollstonecraft, Emily Dickinson, and Georgia O'Keeffe. The table rests on a floor made of tiles on which are inscribed the names of 998 more women (and, accidentally, one man—it turns out Cresilla, the Greek sculptor, was actually a guy named Kresilas). Chicago said the goal of the work was to "end the ongoing cycle of omission in which women were written out of the historical record."

Various criticisms have been and continue to be leveled at the work—that's what art is for, after all—but I love visiting the work, being challenged by its incredible richness and the legacy of each of the guests at Chicago's permanent party. I see the names and think about how much I have to learn from them, how much they have to teach me. I wish I had a seat at this party. Chicago might remind me that I do, if I want one.

At first, when I started thinking about this book, I wanted to write about how to make a great party. But then I realized something: I was more interested in actually throwing a party, introducing people to women I think of as "my friends," even though I've never met any of them, and even though some of them, to be perfectly honest, intimidate the hell out of me. Some of them died before I was born; others passed far more recently. My fantasy of friendship is entirely one-sided, and I find myself wondering if I would have passed muster with some of them.

But writing the book felt like a challenge akin to a fantasy version of that old getting-to-know-you game: If you could have a dinner party with anyone, dead or alive, who would you choose?

My answer is here in *Salty*, though I've cheated and picked nine women instead of one, and some of them would probably bring a guest, too. You may have met some of these women before through their books, art, food, and ideas. Or they may all be strangers to you. That's okay. That's the idea. That's why I've asked you here.

I began this book just weeks after the COVID-19 pandemic caused much of the world to shut down. Staying home, with the act of gathering exactly the one thing we were told *not* to do, I began writing about feasting. One thing I learned during a time of isolation is precisely why I value gatherings so much, and I don't think I'm alone. My hope is that history will show we learned the value of breaking bread and living life alongside one another in this time. And I hope that as you read this, we're in better times.

I've spent some time with each woman, interested especially in how their lives, work, and ideas tell us something about living a life of feasting. Some of them have a lot to say about eating and drinking. Others are experts on friendship, failure, and activism. They wrote novels, led organizations, fought for freedom, raised children, mentored others, paid close attention to the world. When faced with adversity, they refused to knuckle under. They made their mark, and most of all, they *lived*, refusing to simply sleepwalk through an unexamined life.

What I found in them was inspiration for my own life. I think a lot about Laurie Colwin's encouragement to allow myself to fail, Ella Baker's insistence on treating every person with serious attention, Agnès Varda's joyful embrace of discards and leftovers. I am roused by cookbooks, by Elizabeth David's hopeful wit and Edna Lewis's quiet subversion. I am thrilled and disquieted by Octavia Butler's understanding of the human problem, and confronted by Alice B. Toklas's quiet, steely determination to turn meals into art. I am swept along by Maya Angelou's joyfully expansive hope. And I am challenged each day by Hannah Arendt's commitment to friendships, not just as a comfort but as a flinty rock on which to sharpen herself and challenge the powerful.

In each woman I see grace breaking through, enabling them to face an often frightening world and give courage to their readers, their audiences, their communities. I see something I want to be and learn. And I see something that can, in turn, teach us about the tremendous and life-changing power of eating, and drinking, and living.

So now, if you're willing, I'd love for you to join them around my table. We have martinis, and tongue-tingling mineral water, and some nice cheese and pickled vegetables and a big loaf of fresh bread and lovely soft butter. Or if that's not your style, picture whatever you like on this table—you're part of this now. It's our feast, together. Let's make a community. Let's make a world.

## CHAPTER ONE

# EDNA LEWIS

## REWRITING THE STORY

In my earliest days in New York City, I unwittingly tailed one of the greatest food writers of the twentieth century. But I had no idea.

Every weekend, I went to the greenmarket in Union Square, armed with a tote bag and a sense of adventure. Farmers and artisans from upstate regions and New Jersey drove into the city with flats of eggs, bottles of honey, loaves of bread, crates of beets and potatoes and chard and, on a couple lucky weekends every spring, ramps. You could buy apples and apple cider, manchego and smoked sausage, a hunk of beef or a leg of lamb, a duck egg, a pound of coffee roasted a few days ago. Thick tangy yogurt. A giant fennel bulb with waving fronds. A wedge of raspberry banana bread to munch on while you shop. Bring cash.

The Union Square greenmarket is positioned more or less at the center of lower Manhattan, and the market tents stretch up the west side of the square, from 14th to 16th Street. New York University's main buildings are a stone's throw away. There's a giant Whole Foods

Market and a Trader Joe's facing the square, which can be handy if you want to pick up things you can't get at the greenmarket. But it's delightful to just wander through the market and buy a few things for dinner. You'll never have to brave the lines and crush of the stores. And you get to talk to the growers and makers and vendors. I was excited to buy all of their wares. At the time, it felt like everyone was talking about farm-to-table restaurants, the "slow food" movement, and eating seasonally. Seemingly every cookbook and new restaurant cited the groundbreaking Berkeley restaurant Chez Panisse and its visionary owner, Alice Waters, as inspirations.

I was cooking in my own kitchen for the first time, and I had made a new friend who had trained as a chef. So, at the farmers' market, I bought whole chickens and root vegetables and cheese, and she made dinner for a few of us. It was a revelation.

What we didn't know at the time was that the culinary trail we were hiking had been blazed by Edna Lewis. I was a couple decades too late to run into her smiling but imposing figure in that same greenmarket; by the time I got to the city, she was living out her later years in Atlanta. I wouldn't have known who she was at the time, anyhow. Despite her status as one of the century's most important and influential chefs, a revolutionary who refused to be confined to the worlds that were available to Black women in the culinary arts, lots of people have never heard of her. She won major awards and published highly acclaimed books before passing away in 2006. But you're much more likely to have heard of some of her white contemporaries and aco-lytes—Julia Child, for instance, or Alice Waters—than Lewis herself. In a 2017 episode of *Top Chef*, the competing cooks were asked to make a dish that paid homage to Lewis. A number of the professional chefs had no idea who she was. And after the episode aired, her cookbooks saw a spike in sales; the audience hadn't known, either.

But during her lifetime, the culinary world and the vendors at Union Square greenmarket knew her. In 1988, when she was already in her seventies—an extraordinary age to work in the demanding world of a professional kitchen—Lewis was lured back to New York City, where she'd lived previously for many years, to cook at the venerable Brooklyn restaurant Gage & Tollner. She worked there only a few years, but it was a notable moment in the storied institution's history. Lewis worked in Brooklyn but lived in Manhattan, and so, like many chefs, she would go to the Union Square greenmarket to buy ingredients for the restaurant's menu. At a 2013 New School panel on Lewis's legacy, her book editor, the legendary Judith Jones, said that when Lewis walked around the greenmarket, the sellers would call out to her, coaxing her to check out their wares. And she would offer help to anyone who asked how an item might best be prepared.

But her real interest was the freshest, finest, most flavorful food. "She'd walk fifty blocks for a peach," Jones said with a chuckle.

That fresh, juicy peach surely evoked memories for Lewis. She was born in 1916 to a family that, like many Black families in America, lived with painfully recent memories of life during slavery. Her grandfather was one of three freed African American men who, with their families, established a community in Virginia they dubbed Freetown. While enslaved, her grandmother had been a bricklayer. Lewis's grandparents couldn't read or write—teaching an enslaved person to do so was illegal—but in Freetown, they opened their home to a teacher so a school could be established.

Lewis grew up in a large family, situated in a community in which the goals were self-sufficiency, caring for the land, and cooperating with your neighbors. They raised all kinds of animals, fished in the streams, grew crops, and only bought a few necessities from the store. The years moved according to the rhythm and order of the seasons and the feasts that celebrated them. Harvests, holidays, homecomings, changes in the weather—it all meant new things to cook and preserve and butcher and, most importantly, eat.

Memories of cooking at the elbows of her relatives stuck with Lewis, as did those of gathering to eat the fruits of their labor, along with the emotions that went with them. The excitement of butchering pigs in the fall, then blowing their bladders up like balloons with straws and hanging them to dry out for use as Christmas decorations in upcoming weeks. The joy of a good, hearty breakfast before a harvest or butchering or preserving day, the adults adding just a little bourbon to their coffee to fortify them for the work to come. The happiness of seeing far-flung relatives come home for feasts. The bone-weary gladness that comes with a long day spent in the kitchen or the fields, knowing that the fruits of your labor are *yours*, and no one else's. These were the memories that lodged themselves in Lewis's brain.

In 1928, when Edna Lewis was twelve, her father passed away. Money was already tight, and it got tighter when the Depression began. Lewis didn't finish high school, and when she was sixteen she moved to Washington, DC, and then, eventually, to New York City. She worked as a housekeeper, cooking and cleaning, and later she began working as a seamstress. Soon she was known for her skill, her dresses inspired by African styles, and her uncanny knack for copying couture.

But Lewis never got too dazzled by her affluent clients. She married a retired Merchant Marine cook named Steven Kingston, who was active in the Communist Party. It didn't take her long to recognize that, at the time, the party was taking Black people seriously in a way other political parties failed to do, so she joined the Communist Party, too. She set type for the party's paper, *The*

*Daily Worker*, and participated in political demonstrations. Her sense that the capitalist system was not set up for the flourishing of Black people and her memory of the more communal lifestyle of Freetown were always on her mind.

While she worked as a seamstress and participated in political activity, Lewis also drew a circle of friends to herself who appreciated great cooking—namely, *her* cooking. She frequently held dinner parties in her home, to her guests' great appreciation, cooking the foods and recipes she remembered from home: Southern food, by way of Virginia. Outside of the South at the time, Southern-style food was hard to come by, even in New York City. That's a little hard to fathom from our perch in the twenty-first century, when New York's most exclusive brunch spots now often serve shrimp and grits and fried chicken, and when Southern cookbooks dominate the culinary awards landscape.

For many across the United States, Southern food defines American cuisine more than any other region does. But when Lewis started out, Southern food wasn't seen as something refined, certainly not something you'd find on a menu at a fancy restaurant. Chefs at chic city eateries weren't clamoring to serve Southern meals.

At the time, many people also considered the South to be backward, prejudiced, poor, and uneducated, not a place with cuisine worthy of exporting. Official policies regarding segregation in the region—a product of racism in political, governmental, and cultural systems—certainly contributed to the perception. European cuisine was what you aspired to. Julia Child was introducing home cooks to French dishes, not American food.

The American South has always been more than just what other people think of it, of course. And many of those who contributed to that perception, who considered the South to be backward, were participating in systems that perpetuated *de facto* segregation elsewhere—including in northern cities like New York, where racial discrimination in eateries was still commonplace until the 1960s.

Still, roaming Southerners in New York longed for the food of their home kitchens, and it wasn't easy to come by, for a fairly simple reason: Southern food was developed by Black people, usually Black women, first as enslaved people and then as domestic help. But with widespread illiteracy throughout the early twentieth century, the recipes weren't often written down. Instead, they were passed down through oral tradition, or through community cookbooks in which their white employers passed off the recipes of "the help" as their own. There were very few Black people—certainly no Black women—heading up kitchens at New York's restaurants.

As a Virginian, Lewis learned Southern cooking that was inflected by French influences, thanks to the many Virginians (like Thomas Jefferson) who spent years in France and returned with preferences developed at French tables. Her kind of cooking wasn't easy to find outside of Virginia. Guests at her New York table, though, were fortunate to enjoy what she was making— pies, preserves, blanc mange, and certainly, fried chicken.

One of the guests at Lewis's dinner table was a young man named John Nicholson, an antiques dealer. In 1948, he opened a café on the Upper East Side, on East 58th Street, and called it Café Nicholson. He asked Lewis to be the chef.

It was rare for a woman to be a restaurant chef at the time. It was exceptionally rare for a Black woman to take that position. And Lewis wasn't just the chef; she was an equal partner in the business, which was unheard of.

Café Nicholson was a hit and became a haunt for famous New Yorkers, many of whom—like Tennessee Williams and William Faulkner—were white Southerners surprised to find Southern cuisine on the Upper East Side. The restaurant's European-style decor mixed with Lewis's cooking attracted literati and glitterati: Marlon Brando, Eleanor Roosevelt, Richard Avedon, Gloria Vanderbilt, Gore Vidal, Jean Renoir, and Marlene Dietrich were all happy customers. They feasted on roasted chickens and chocolate soufflés, all cooked by Lewis from her own recipes. While her simple and elegant menu didn't have biscuits on it, Alabama-raised Truman Capote used to bug Lewis to make him some anyhow. She was the chef and a partner for the café until her departure in 1954.

〰〰〰〰〰〰〰〰〰〰〰〰

It's not entirely clear why she left. Some of it may have had to do with Kingston, her husband, who was thoroughly committed to the Communist cause. That's how Nicholson remembered it when, in 2004, he told the *New York Times* as much. "He always used to say, 'This restaurant should be for ordinary people on the street. You're catering to capitalists,'" Nicholson said, adding, "It was such a bore."

Lewis and Kingston's move to New Jersey to become pheasant farmers was a short-lived experiment. One night, the whole flock died from a mysterious illness, and that was that. They returned to New York.

Back in the city, Lewis opened a restaurant in Harlem that lasted only a year or two. Despite her reputation as the chef at Café Nicholson, new jobs weren't forthcoming, particularly for a Black woman. So she took catering gigs and cooked for friends, while also taking a job as a docent at the American Museum of Natural History. And she co-wrote a cookbook with the socialite Evangeline Peterson, titled *The Edna Lewis Cookbook*, which was published in 1972.

The recipes in *The Edna Lewis Cookbook* were relatively simple, based on the kinds of food that Lewis served at Café Nicholson. The book is adamant about using fresh, high-quality ingredients.

"Our aim has been to present a cookbook with recipes for the kind of food that we feel people really eat and that are not too complicated to prepare," the authors note in the introduction. They exhort the reader to take care with their shopping: "The use of fresh ingredients of fine quality is as important to the final results of a recipe as is care in preparation." The recipes are arranged into sections by season and type of meal (luncheons, dinners, buffets), without much commentary other than notes about selecting the right kind of curry or what a perfectly roasted duck looks like.

It was a groundbreaking book in its own right, proposing that many Southern-style recipes are as worthy of record as other cuisine in New York City and beyond, and situating those foods in the gourmet landscape. Food figures as prominent as M.F.K. Fisher and James Beard praised it. It was a good book, but some still thought it lacked character and voice. That richness would come with her next book.

In the spring of 1972, as *The Edna Lewis Cookbook* was heading for publication, Lewis met Judith Jones. Jones was (and probably still is) the key figure in American cookbook publishing; she was Julia Child's editor. Jones's boss at the time knew Peterson and suggested that Jones meet with Peterson and Lewis to talk about their next project. As they spoke, Jones had an idea: What if Lewis wrote a book that blended her stories of her home in Freetown with recipes based on her memories? Would she be willing to try that?

She was. Peterson and Lewis started writing again, but when they returned with pages, Jones was disappointed, feeling as if Lewis's voice had been stripped out. Peterson recognized that her role didn't serve the book or Lewis's voice. She decided to withdraw from the project, and in concert with Jones, Lewis got to work. She'd go to Jones's apartment and tell her stories about the people, the land, the foods, the gatherings, with Jones prodding her for details. Then Lewis would go home and write those stories down on yellow legal pads. Lewis's twelve-year-old niece, Nina Williams, helped her by typing up the pages.

Published in 1976, *The Taste of Country Cooking* became a landmark in American food writing. It reads like a memoir as much as a cookbook. Lewis begins by telling the story of Freetown: "The name was adopted because the first residents had all been freed from chattel slavery and they wanted to be known as a town of Free People." In loving, lyrical prose, she wrote of the spirit of community, pride, and cooperation, the affection that the adults had for the children, and the hard work they all did together.

And she recounts in the introduction how something very specific and wonderful stitched together the families of Freetown. "Whenever I go back to visit my sisters and brothers, we relive old times, remembering the past. And when we share again in gathering wild strawberries, canning, rendering lard, finding walnuts, picking persimmons, making fruitcake, I realize how much the bond that held us had to do with food," she wrote.

"Above all," she concludes, "I want to share with everyone who may read this a time and a place that is so very dear to my heart."

As in *The Edna Lewis Cookbook*, the chapters are arranged seasonally, this time beginning with spring and ending in winter. Each chapter opens with reflections on the joys of the season, the things they anticipated—shad fish at breakfast in the spring, homemade ice cream and fresh melons in the summer, shucking corn in the fall, chopping nuts and dried fruits for Christmas fruitcake in the winter. Within each chapter are a number of menus with names like "A Late Spring Lunch After Wild-Mushroom Picking," "Sunday Revival Dinner," "Morning-After-Hog-Butchering Breakfast," and "A Dinner Celebrating the Last of the Barnyard Fowl." Lewis recalls all of these from the vantage point of a child—after all, she left

Freetown when she was a teenager. She weaves in memories of family members visiting from afar, long tables spread with white cloths in the churchyard, the excitement of her father bringing the cattle home from the community pasture after a summer of grazing. Her reflections evoke the uncomplicated perspective of a child who knows herself to be loved and feels her place in the world.

But of course, the adult Lewis was writing the book, and though at times readers have viewed it as simply nostalgic, it's also quietly revolutionary, shattering barriers that Lewis's first cookbook hadn't touched. The political activist and "fast-talking" woman her niece remembered didn't indulge in sentimentality. Some of Lewis's seemingly matter-of-fact statements about food and gathering have deep roots in the story of Black communities in early twentieth-century Virginia. Her "simple" remembrances actually say volumes about the way they faced economic and cultural oppression, which forced them to grasp for self-sufficiency and to live off the land.

Historian Sara Franklin, who edited the 2018 essay collection *Edna Lewis: At the Table with an American Original*, remarked that *The Taste of Country Cooking* was "a corrective Black history disguised as a cookbook. An amazing book, a Trojan horse!" She noted that "the brilliance of [*The Taste of Country Cooking*] in terms of form is that it paired food—which everyone likes—with these truths that are both painful and went against the grain of popular narratives of American Black culture."

Reading *The Taste of Country Cooking*, it's remarkable how lasting the recipes are, and with a handful of exceptions, it's easy to find all of the ingredients in a supermarket today. The only outliers are extremely local foods, the sort you could catch in the wilds of Virginia. That's unusual for a cookbook published in the 1970s. You'll meet Laurie Colwin at our table soon; her

*Home Cooking* books, as delightful as they are to read, are full of recipes (the one that always gets me is "chicken in chicken glaze") brimming with ingredients that don't sound appetizing to the modern ear. Even my beloved Robert Farrar Capon, author of the great work of theology and food *The Supper of the Lamb*, hands over suggestions in his 1969 volume that today sound truly wild. (So much mayonnaise!)

But Lewis did no such thing. The book could be published tomorrow with virtually no alterations. It holds true. Her ingredients are chickens, yeast, ham, butter, strawberries, collard greens, honey, and the best baking powder you can buy (if you can't make it yourself). Strikingly, there's very little mention of the specific nutritional or "healthful" quality of the foods, except when she's speaking of dishes that draw a direct line back to her African ancestors. In her recipe on the "Preparation of Leafy Greens"— which could be "Kale, Rape, Mustard, Lamb's-Quarters, Wild Watercress, Purslane, Broccoli Rabb or Turnip-Top Leaves, Beet Tops"—she notes that they "need not be greasy." And then she points out where this recipe came from: "Some varieties of leafy greens we would gather and cook every day, mostly because we knew instinctively that they were of nutritional value—an instinct that comes from our African heritage, I'm sure. Even though nutrition was our major concern, we always prepared them in a manner that made them taste very delicious." (That method involved adding some bacon and garlic.)

This pointed reference is a rare one in the book, and it's hard not to see it as counteracting popular myths about what Black Southerners ate in the 1970s. The perception that they were eating greasy, unhealthful foods was a widespread racist meme repeated by whites, particularly in the North. But Lewis challenges that notion. Not only was her community interested in nutrition, she wrote, but nutrition was built into their DNA, thanks to their ancestors. And contrary to what some people would have thought of as "health food" in those early days of the back-to-the-land movement, healthy food to Edna Lewis didn't mean bad-tasting food. She believed food could be both healthy and flavorful at once.

There's more in the book that suggests Lewis was slipping in radical notions alongside the recipes and memories. In a 2015 profile for the *New York Times*, the food journalist Francis Lam pointed out that Lewis takes care as she evokes the image of butchered hogs hanging in the yard. The day after the slaughter, Lewis writes, "my brothers and sisters and I would rush out before breakfast to see the hogs hanging from the scaffolds like giant statues. The hogs looked beautiful. They were glistening white inside with their lining of fat, and their skin was almost translucent." Lam notes that two years after Lewis was born, a Black man named Charles Allie Thompson was lynched in the nearby town of Culpeper. "A mob hung him from a tree after claims that he raped a white woman," Lam writes. "He had been seen asking her to help with butchering, at hog-killing time."

"Whether Lewis intended to imbue her hog-killing scene with such references, it became impossible for me to read *The Taste of Country Cooking* without a sense of the wider setting of her story and how she chose to tell it without terror, how she refused to let the past, her past, be defined by anyone else but her," Lam writes.

*The Taste of Country Cooking* makes this much clear: that spirit of self-definition is something Lewis learned as a child from watching her family. In the book, there are celebration feasts for Emancipation Day and Homecoming, both of which were woven into the life of Freetown. The Emancipation Day dinner menu included steamed wild rice, green bean salad with sliced tomatoes, Parker House rolls, grape jelly made from wild grapes, plum tart, stewed quince, cookies, and coffee, and it was anchored by "Guinea Fowl in Casserole." Lewis pointedly ensures that we understand that this is a meal intended to connect the celebrants to the broader African diaspora:

> Guineas were an integral part of every barnyard in Freetown. They were cultivated because of their watchdog quality; they always made a big fuss whenever any stranger appeared. The guinea fowl has its origin in West Africa and their African link was passed on from generation to generation by African-Americans. They were eaten only on rare occasions and had to be shot, as they lived in trees and roamed the countryside. They were treated like any game birds.

Lewis and her family knew that there was always a reason to be more than a little wary of strangers. A wary, watching bird made for a perfect and uneasy Emancipation Day feast. Notably, there's no recipe for or mention of Thanksgiving in *The Taste of Country Cooking*—a holiday not celebrated in Freetown.

Franklin, the food historian, says Lewis was radical, but "in the other sense, radical meaning 'of the root,' fundamental." As I read those words, I hear an echo of Ella Baker, another Black Virginian, born thirteen years before Lewis, also to a family with fresh memories of slavery and a commitment to community, education, family, and justice. (You'll meet her shortly.) In her organizing to fight on behalf of Black Southerners, Baker focused on the wisdom of communities and the need for the poor to drive their own change. Lewis lived this. And she was convinced that that wisdom was tied to the land, to caring for the gifts of the earth, and to the love that stitches a community together.

"She was interested in a life that centered and attended to what's essential, what's fundamental to our existence as human beings: food, mutuality, maintenance, care," Franklin says. "She had a reverence for the natural world, and a deep devotion to responsible stewardship of land that was *way* ahead of her time." The back-to-the-land and environmental movements often see white writers like Rachel Carson, Wendell Berry, and Wes Jackson as their elder statespeople. But Lewis rightly deserves this mantle, as she was exploring these same concerns in some cases decades before others—just without the media hype. "Lewis was saying a lot of the same things, just from a different angle," Franklin says. "She, too, was calling for the same tender treatment of land in a way that, to me, echoes an indigenous perspective, one not grounded in private ownership and economic gain."

Some of Lewis's concern for the land was due to her political commitments, but it also flowed from her lived experience in Freetown. "Lewis took the story of rural Black people, formerly enslaved Black people, and owned it as a story of confidence and beauty," Lam writes. "She didn't have an easy life, even in her Freetown years. Her family suffered through two stillborn children and two more who died young of pneumonia. But she chose to see, and to show us, beauty; and under the shadow of oppression and slavery, that is a political act."

||||||||||||||||||||||||||||||||

In the years that followed the publication of *The Taste of Country Cooking*, Lewis wrote two other cookbooks: *In Pursuit of Flavor* and *The Gift of Southern Cooking*, the latter coauthored with her protégé and friend Scott Peacock. She worked as a chef at various restaurants in the South and in New York, including Gage & Tollner. She founded the Society for the Revival and Preservation of Southern Food, the predecessor to the Southern Foodways Alliance. She won the James Beard Living Legend Award and several Lifetime Achievement Awards. The culinary world saw her as an important figure, someone who established Southern American cooking not just as legitimate but as a key cuisine that insisted on the centrality of Black Americans and the broader African diaspora.

In 2008, two years after her death, *Gourmet* magazine published a newly discovered unpublished essay of Lewis's titled "What Is Southern?" It reads like poetry:

> Southern is a bowl of shrimp paste, rich in butter, shrimp, Sherry, spices, and lemon juice. Blended to a soft consistency and served over a plate of grits, a delicious breakfast treat. Southern is a barbecued pig that was cooked for hours and served with a tomato- or vinegar-based sauce, as well as coleslaw, potato salad, baked beans, hush puppies, and iced tea. Southern is a bowl of homemade peach ice cream, served during the peach season. Southern is Richard Wright and his "Bright and Morning Star." Southern is an oyster roast. Guests are presented with white gloves for shucking and pots of melted butter. Southern is leftover pieces of boiled ham trimmed and added to a saucepan of heavy cream set on the back of the stove to mull and bring out the ham flavor, then spooned over hot biscuits, with poached eggs on the side.

Every paragraph reads like this—rich sensory descriptions that make your mouth water, mixed with names of chefs and writers and memories of her youth in Freetown. Lewis defines Southern as the experience of an emancipated people and their descendants, a cultural and culinary heritage to be proud of, a distinctly American culture, and as she offers definitions, readers are reminded she is refusing to be defined by anyone but herself.

That's what is so incredible about Edna Lewis. But while white friends like Judith Jones and Scott Peacock were close and valuable to her, her legacy never seemed to reach far enough for white chefs—even those who should be in the know—who grabbed onto farm-to-table seasonal cooking only to realize they were following in her footsteps. Alice Waters has frequently acknowledged her debt to Lewis; in her preface to the 30th anniversary edition of *The Taste of Country Cooking*, published the year Lewis died, Waters writes that "she was far more than the doyenne of Southern cooking. She was, and she remains, an inspiration to all of us who are striving to protect both biodiversity and cultural diversity by cooking real food in season and honoring our heritage through the ritual of the table." Franklin notes that Waters "definitely didn't do enough to turn the spotlight on Lewis" during Lewis's lifetime "in a way I think is unforgivable, and also very typical, of white American culture." Indigenous communities and communities of color often practiced sustainable agriculture and "farm-to-table" eating long before white American chefs adapted the practices and called them "new."

In my days of wandering the Union Square greenmarket, I knew none of this. Learning to cook, for me, has been a process of understanding that women like Edna Lewis, like the women gathered around this dinner table, have defined and refined what it means to "eat well," often over and against social and cultural perceptions of their cultures and their food. Women like Edna Lewis challenge orthodoxies. And importantly, they define food and root it in how we live, and how we come together—they root it in love.

Edna Lewis's courage to use food as a way to challenge and rewrite perceptions of her community was striking; her ability to change the way Americans eat was virtually unparalleled. And she did it all while asking her readers to come for a walk with her through her memories of Freetown, a place that freed chattel slaves established and named because they wanted everyone to know that they were, at last, free.

# FEAST
## Boiled Greens à la Freetown, with Pork

The greatest feasts are found in Lewis's own cookbooks, so I hope this small taste will lure you toward her magnificent books.

I grew up eating lots of greens—kale and collards and chard and beet greens. And so I am especially attracted to Lewis's recipe for greens, which I have made often. They're delicious. In *The Taste of Country Cooking*, she writes out her recipes narratively; this is simply my attempt to adapt this recipe into standard cookbook style, with greens that are easily accessible in most parts of the country and a few preferences of my own. All credit to Lewis and her African ancestors.

Depending on how much you like greens, this makes enough for two or so, with some extra pork left over.

## For the Stock

1-lb. piece of cured bacon or smoked pork shoulder

Water to cover the pork

## For the Greens

1 big bunch of kale, or about 10 oz. if you are buying it bagged

¼ c. olive oil

1 clove garlic, minced

1. Put the pork into a saucepan or a dutch oven and cover with water, then place it on the burner and turn it on high.

2. Lewis's recipe says "Boil until done," which is not incredibly clear. Your goal is to get its internal temperature to 150 degrees, which should take around 20 minutes once it really gets boiling; the larger the piece of pork, the longer it will take. Your meat thermometer is your friend.

3. While it's boiling, wash your greens thoroughly and strip the leaves off the stalks.

4. When the pork reaches the right internal temperature, take it out. Then plunge the greens into the boiling stock. They'll shrink down impressively as they cook. Stir them to make sure they all get blanched.

5. Lewis writes, "Press the greens down lightly in the stock and cook them fast but gently for no more than 15 to 20 minutes. Cook uncovered, which prevents them from turning brown. Remove them from the burner and let them sit in the broth, partly covered now. Gently reheat them and then drain them when ready to serve."

6. Lewis's recipe ends there. You can serve them right now, and they'll have flavor thanks to the pork stock. But she also mentions a way to cook certain kinds of greens, like broccoli rabe. I like this preparation for kale, too, so here's a modified version of what to do next: Drain the kale well, squeezing it to shed some of the extra broth. Over high heat, place a wide, shallow pan (like a skillet) and add the olive oil. When it's hot, add the garlic and fry it for less than a

minute. Then add the greens (it will sputter because of the broth clinging to the greens, so be careful). Stir the greens in the pan until they're coated with the garlicky oil, then remove from heat and serve. You might want to add a little salt and pepper, too.

7. Serve the greens with the pork (sliced, maybe with mustard), and maybe some biscuits. You can find recipes for those in *The Taste of Country Cooking*.

# More Salt with Edna Lewis

*The Edna Lewis Cookbook, The Taste of Country Cooking, In Pursuit of Flavor,* and *The Gift of Southern Cooking*: Lewis's cookbooks are a rich introduction to her and her work. They're each worth reading on their own, but if you can only choose one, choose *The Taste of Country Cooking.*

"What Is Southern?" (originally published in Gourmet magazine, and available in full at giarts.org/article/what-southern): Lewis's article about what "Southern" means is essential reading—it's about food, culture, race, heritage, literature, Blackness, and more. The piece was accidentally lost in the *Gourmet* magazine offices. Two years after her death, the editors found and published it. It's a lyrical encapsulation of everything Lewis was about.

*Edna Lewis: At the Table with an Original,* edited by Sara B. Franklin: A collection of essays by scholars, chefs, and historians that extend and also challenge common perceptions of who Lewis was and what she stood for.

## CHAPTER TWO

# LAURIE COLWIN
## ORDINARY, MESSED-UP FEASTS

I once got my hands on a good lamb rump from a local farm, a cut I'd never roasted before, slightly too big for my husband and me to eat by ourselves. So a friend who lives down the street came over for a little feast. He brought his teenage daughter, a vegetarian. I prepared a roasting pan of root vegetables in her honor. But the main event, big enough for three hungry adults, was the lamb rump.

I had read plenty about the dangers of overcooking a lamb's rump, and so, being fond of rare meat myself, I monitored the cut's progress carefully. (In the food world there's not much worse than overcooked meat.) So, first I pan-fried it on the stovetop in a wide cast-iron pan we inherited from my in-laws. Then I slid it into the oven to "finish" it, as Jamie Oliver instructs—my reasoning being that an English chef would most likely know how to make lamb delicious. As it roasted next to a pan containing chunks of carrot, slices of red onion, and hunks of potatoes, we ate Danish blue cheese our friends had brought from the local co-op, spread on oblong slices of baguette piled onto a platter. We hovered over the wide counter that separates kitchen from living room in our small apartment, chattering and watching the clock tick down the minutes till the roasting oven would have finished its task.

Finally it was time to remove the lamb from its cast-iron nest, a task that can only be accomplished with a surprising amount of upper-body strength. I braced, hauled it out, and set it on the stovetop to rest for a few minutes. Then I carefully transferred it to a cutting board and sliced in.

Jamie Oliver writes that it should be "blushing pink" in the center, and indeed, the end slices were. But by the time I had hit the one-third point, the blushing pink had turned more fuchsia, and halfway in it looked like a crime had taken place—blood spilled across the white cutting board and ran into the moat carved into the cutting board's edges for situations exactly like this one.

I stared in consternation. "Well, it's supposed to be rare!" I said uncertainly.

Sensing my alarm, my friend replied, "Whatever you think." Hidden in his smile but reflected in his eyes I could see just a hint of panic.

I could not do it. I could not force completely raw lamb meat on my husband and our friend, especially not in front of a teenage vegetarian munching happily on a tender carrot. I repositioned the pan, heated it over a burner, finished slicing the lamb, and fried the pieces briefly on both sides, upon which they took on a slightly pinkish-gray hue. I had not thought to make a gravy of the juices, but now it was just too late. The meat was tough, not the melty, juicy, savory morsels I'd imagined. And though the men each gallantly ate a few medallions of grayish lamb rump, we soon poured stiff drinks and joined our vegetarian in feasting on the vegetables and the rest of the Danish blue.

I don't screw up feasts very often, so this incident sticks in my head, one of my failures that I still puzzle over. Not that I haven't tempted Lady Fate plenty by doing the one thing you're not supposed to do: try out new recipes on company. I am pathologically incapable of sticking to the familiar when entertaining. So far it hasn't caused too much chaos, but occasions like the Lamb Rump Incident remind me not to get too cocky.

But—and hear me out—maybe being a little cocky in the kitchen is okay, if you have the right patron saint to look out for you, pat you on the head, and say it's just fine, it happens to the best of us. For me, that saint is Laurie Colwin, the novelist of domestic life and guiding light to several generations of bookish home cooks through her two essay collections. All of Colwin's novels and short story collections boast airily abstract titles, like *Passion and Affect*, *Another Marvelous Thing*, *Family Happiness*, and *Happy All the Time*, words that sound as much like the titles of self-help manuals for successful living as what they really are: tales of marriages, families, affairs, friendships, and individuals who live comfortable lives but wish to be living *other* sorts of comfortable lives.

Her food writing, though, is what has endeared her to the hearts of readers who were too young to read her before she passed in 1992, leaving behind her book-publisher husband, Juris Jurjevics, and a young child.

Colwin died of a heart attack at age forty-eight, a fact that colors her essays on cooking. They're collected in books with much more literal titles than the ones her volumes of fiction bear: *Home Cooking: A Writer in the Kitchen* (published in 1988) and *More Home Cooking: A Writer Returns to the Kitchen* (posthumously published in 1993). She's always writing of the challenges and joys of feeding people in an age when everyone has a dietary preference or restriction—vegans, people with sensitive stomachs, friends on "no fat" diets, which, when read in our present age of butter coffee and keto diets, feels hilariously dated. But an entire chapter entitled "Without Salt" introduces Colwin's penchant for salt and how she figured out how to flavor things without it, after her doctor told her she needed to cut it out or she'd end up with hypertension. She figured it out. "I am now a better, slightly thinner person because of this regime," she writes.

Regardless of some foreshadowing, reading Colwin on cooking is life-giving, even if you don't intend to make anything she recommends. Her recipes are not terribly interesting or original or, in some cases, very appealing. I will never make "scarlet eggs," and I would probably turn to a less colloquially written source if I had a hankering to make plum jam. I've also made bread enough times to know that her recipe, which she characterizes (in a chapter titled "Bread Baking Without Agony") as one that "unlike most things in life . . . adjusts to you," would probably not work very well for people who can't sense by touch whether the dough has developed enough gluten to avoid becoming a dense brick.

No matter. What's joyous about Colwin's food writing is its chatty "you've got this" voice, her sense that cooking is fun and nice and a great thing to do, and if you mess something up occasionally, that's fine. It just means you'll try it again another day. She writes of dinner parties she's given with humor and a wink, reminding you that your excuses are in vain, because *she* started out hosting dinner in her twenties in Greenwich Village, in a "little one-room apartment a little larger than the *Columbia Encyclopedia*":

> Of course there was no space for anything like a dining room table, something quite unnecessary as there was no dining room. When I was alone I ate at my desk, or on a tray in bed. When company came I opened a folding card table with a cigarette burn in its leatherette

top. This object was stored in a slot between my countertop and my extremely small closet. Primitive as my kitchen arrangements were, I had company for dinner fairly often.

In the very next paragraph, Colwin goes on to tell us about her first dinner party in the apartment, for which she invited two college friends over—both named Alice, dubbed "the Alices"— and tried to serve them beef fondue, a catastrophe that ended with them sautéing whatever steak hadn't turned into "little lumps of rubbery coal," then going to a local bar for hamburgers and french fries.

Most confident home cooks have this kind of story up their sleeve, the product of years of figuring out what's worth doing when you're trying to feed your friends (pizza, soup, a roasted chicken) and what's almost never a good idea (anything with the word *soufflé* in the name). Several times throughout both books, Colwin recounts with glee the stories of dinner parties she went to at *other* people's houses that were mildly catastrophic. One time, a dour friend of a friend announced to his guests before dinner that he wasn't sure if there would be enough for all of them, then served them inedible boiled beef, and they were in the odd position of being grateful that he had, indeed, been correct. Another time, a well-meaning friend served some kind of food item that arrived at the table served in a whole, carved-out pumpkin and which she announced was an "Argentine dish!":

At these words I felt a little snake of unhappy anticipation crawl up my neck.

From the bowels of this pumpkin came forth a strange substance that was neither soup nor stew and contained overcooked meat and undercooked eggplant. I wondered how this had been done and realized the meat and eggplant had been cooked separately. We sat at an enormous table and drank a vast quantity of expensive wine.

I do wonder if Colwin's friends read her accounts of their failures and felt betrayed. On the other hand, what did they expect when they invited a writer to dinner and served mush in a pumpkin tureen?

The beauty of Colwin's writing—whether it's about food or fiction—is that her huge, generous heart is always on display. For her, these screw-ups aren't (usually) a measuring rod for whether the cook is a good person, but a happy reminder that the best-laid plans of mice and men can go horribly awry, and that shouldn't hold us back from trying to love one another regardless.

Colwin is opinionated and self-critical and just as willing to make lighthearted fun of herself as she is of anyone else. She has whole chapters on her catastrophes, which she deems "the result of inexperience, overreaching, intimidation, and self-absorption": brownies so dense she couldn't cut through them, a cataclysmic pudding, a red snapper she roasted for Jurjevics before they were married that came out of the oven looking "like Hieronymus Bosch's vision of hell." Years after she passed away, Jurjevics told the *New York Times* that "she was a great cook but the fiascos were kind of fabulous. She cooked haggis once that was like the advertisement for *Alien*, with the cracked egg."

Her sense of genuine delight in the frailties and foibles of humanity goes far beyond kitchen catastrophes. The best word I can think of for Colwin's novels is *comforting*, a word I don't frequently attach to art I actually like, but in this case I find it to be perfect. They're about ordinary women with rich interior lives for whom the pressures of ordinary existence—dealing with a lecherous boss, or caring for a whirling household of two kids and a hardworking husband and a mother who likes to call and judge you—are starting to be a lot.

Her stories aren't moralistic fables in which people must learn a lesson and resolve to be better. In Colwin's novels, nobody does anything explosive or lurid, even if we discover in chapter 3 they're actually having a quiet extramarital affair. Nobody is murdered, and nothing gets blown up. Instead, they keep living, and what they learn, for the most part, is something about themselves. Reading her novels, it's easy to see the connection between the cook who wryly recounts cooking disasters and the author who gives her characters a lot of grace.

In her 1982 novel *Family Happiness*—a title Colwin swiped from Leo Tolstoy—Polly, our heroine, is the mother of two and the wife of a kind but somewhat distracted man. They are well-off, living the kind of middle-class life that was still available in 1982 to a single-income home, even one in New York City. (Polly has a part-time job working in literacy education, but it's more of a passion than a necessity.) Her parents and siblings live in Manhattan as well, and they have brunch together every Sunday at her parents' house.

Polly is the center of gravity for her family, though none of them see that; she is the steady one, the responsible one, while the rest of them are faintly ridiculous. One of her brothers is a stern and ascetic killjoy; another lives a carefree life of childish pursuits with his wife downtown; and Polly's parents are wealthy and sure of their own greatness, even though her father is uptight about everything and her mother is the sort of person who consistently gets basic facts wrong, then becomes offended when Polly tries to correct her. She constantly tells her daughter that her part-time job is making Polly neglect her (perfectly fine and well-adjusted) children.

A little way into the book, we discover that Polly sort of fell backward into an affair with an artist named Lincoln, and she is at a total loss for what to do about it, having no real idea how she ended up in this position or why. It has little effect on her everyday life—with the children in school and her husband busy with work all the time, she has time on her hands. And Lincoln, who has a passion for aloneness only a middle-aged bachelor can summon, both loves Polly with all his heart and yet has no interest in tearing her away from her family.

That's the state of things throughout the whole novel, and when reading it, what's most surprising is that the revelation of Polly's affair is not played as sensational or racy. Instead, Colwin lets it be almost banal. In the narrative, it's ultimately a way for Polly to realize that the pressure she's put on herself to achieve perfection in her family life, solely on her own power, is going to kill her if she keeps it up. But Colwin's goal in the novel isn't to punish Polly and make an example of her. The novel ends in a surprising place, and the characters' relationships to one another shift only a little, mostly in positive ways, but the biggest change is inside Polly.

Throughout *Family Happiness*, Colwin constructs her characters primarily through their attitudes toward food. Polly's father is a hoot, and "funny about food." For him, "everything, from vegetables to standing ribs of beef, should be washed with soap and water before cooking." Eggs must be scrubbed before they're boiled, and orange juice has to be squeezed fresh, not because it tastes better but because "harmful metals leached into juice from cans." Wendy, Polly's mother, a nervous and deeply particular woman, "was not very good about mechanical things, and thus she had chosen what Polly considered to be the most complicated method of making coffee," a Silex. Wendy is confounded by the Silex's two-globe construction, Colwin writes, but insists on using it anyway.

Perhaps as a consequence of being her finicky parents' daughter, Polly is a homebody, and the food she likes best, we're told, is "nursery food. She fed her children shepherd's pie, mashed potatoes, deviled chicken, vegetable fritters, hush puppies, Queen of Puddings, and apple crisp"—practically a duplicate of *Home Cooking*'s table of contents. Polly's husband, Henry, admires "a more complicated cuisine," which Polly is happy to provide: "fresh ham stuffed with pistachios, carpetbagger steak, and veal, ham, and egg pie." He never demands anything, but Polly feels both pleasure and obligation in making it for him, something that, eventually, he tells her she must relax about—he loves her no matter what she feeds him. In contrast, Lincoln and Polly eat simple lunches together in his studio: "bread, cheese, butter, a bunch of grapes, a bottle of red wine, and coffee."

At brunch one Sunday, Polly tells her sister-in-law that she loves to cook, "but when you cook all the time for four people the object is getting it done. I often forget how beautiful vegetables are. Carrots, for instance." That Polly misses the beauty of things in the everyday rush to get them done is something she's just starting to understand, and it is what she spends the rest of the book learning to do: to stop and contemplate the carrots.

In Colwin's final novel, *A Big Storm Knocked It Over*, the protagonist, Jane Louise, is a young woman with a boss who unrelentingly hits on her and every other woman who walks through the office; a new and wonderfully sweet husband named Teddy; and a best friend named Edie, whose family cannot quite bring themselves to approve of her long-term partner Mokie because he is Black. Edie and Mokie are also business partners—caterers, in fact, who work for a preposterously exacting woman named Mrs. Teagarden, whose outlandish ideas about what constitutes a proper society spread send Jane Louise and Edie into fits of laughter, even if Mrs. Teagarden drives them nuts. Mrs. Teagarden, known only through her food, is a symbol of everything they don't want to be: stuffy and uptight, driven by fashion rather than flavor. She reminds the book's young people of their parents. Like Polly in *Family Happiness*, all four have parents who are difficult to be around. But unlike Polly, Jane Louise, in the first blush of her new marriage, has the pluck to convince her husband to spend the holidays without their families.

Published in 1993, a year after Colwin died, *A Big Storm Knocked It Over* is the chronicle of a young woman who doesn't have a lot of external problems but must discover how to be an adult while navigating the first few years of marriage, pregnancy, and care of a newborn. It's Colwin's most mature work of fiction, and it reads like a book written by a woman who's finally figured out what was most important for her to learn in her youth: that the family we choose is just as important as the family we are born into, and that learning to trust the former to support you while you try to love the latter is of vital importance to being an adult.

The most memorable scene for me in *A Big Storm Knocked It Over* comes during Jane Louise and Teddy's first Christmas together. They fantasize for a while about escaping New York for somewhere warm, but money is a little tight, and instead, with Edie and Mokie, they head for somewhere even colder: Vermont, where they spend the holiday at a picturesque lodge owned by an older couple named the Schuldes. They laze around, doing very little, the only guests at the inn, until they are startled on Christmas Eve when friends and family of the Schuldes suddenly start piling into the inn for supper and evening skating. Thankfully, guests of the inn are also invited. Their spread is one worth reproducing in full:

> They stood in the living room, drinking hot cider,
> until the doors to the dining room were pulled back

to reveal the kind of table Edie said Mrs. Teagarden would have paid several hundred thousand dollars to have someone fix up for her. On the large sideboard were three roast ducks, a glazed ham, an enormous glass dish containing a mountain of beet and herring salad, greens, roast potatoes, and a gigantic Christmas cake.

"This is the most beautiful thing I've ever seen," Edie said.

The unexpected circumstances make Jane Louise feel "almost panicky," but they're all feasting together, and feasting is a language she can understand. So Jane Louise begins to relax. After dinner, they all go outside and skate on the pond under the starlight, drinking hot chocolate and declaring this Christmas with strangers—with found family—to be the best Christmas they have ever had.

Like Polly, Jane Louise's task throughout the book is not to change her behavior to acquiesce to the demands of her family or Teddy's, but to try to live in the midst of them while not losing herself entirely. It's the sort of story repeated frequently throughout Colwin's fiction, suggesting a project many readers can relate to: embracing the genuine love of home, the pleasure of creation and cooking, and the good life you've constructed for yourself without becoming a shadow to everyone else around you. Sometimes, for Colwin's characters, that means making a decision that seems decidedly selfish to other characters, usually someone's mother. Sometimes it means dropping the perfect-woman facade and letting her husband know she hasn't got the world by the tail. (There's always a gulf between the men and the women in Colwin's fiction, who are mostly white and well-enough off, and there's rarely a relationship that isn't traditional and heterosexual.) But for most people, living ordinary lives in which not that much happens, the need to accept one's imperfections and impulses, mysterious even to the person who has them, is what Colwin suggests living is all about.

And Colwin never judges her imperfect characters. Just the opposite. She loves them unconditionally, even the silly ones. Like the people who give disastrous dinner parties—including Colwin herself—she sees them, with all of their foibles, and still welcomes them to her feast.

This nonjudgmental attitude toward characters makes Colwin feel like the friend at a cocktail party who hears about something you did and, instead of shaming you or acting shocked, asks you how you feel about it and gets you another glass of wine. (That kind of friend also populates her books, of course.)

And that same voice narrates her books on cooking, which is probably why they're so lovely and comforting to those of us who feel compelled to lay a welcoming spread, but might worry about screwing up. It's all part of the process of growth, one that will never end as long as we keep on living. In the introduction to *More Home Cooking*, published the year after she died, she notes:

> These are hard times for people who like to eat, who like to cook, and who hate to do both but need to. Our present economic system leaves us pressed, drained, exhausted . . . And yet we still need sustenance, and contact. We need time to defuse, to contemplate. Just as in sleep our brains relax and give us dreams, so at some time in the day we need to disconnect, reconnect, and look around us.

That's where meals come in—ordinary feasts to be had at home with some people we love, by choice or by birth:

We must march into the kitchen, en famille or with a friend, and find some easy, heartwarming things to make from scratch, and even if it is but once a week, we must gather at the table, alone or with friends or with lots of friends or with one friend, and eat a meal together. We know that without food we would die. Without fellowship life is not worth living.

Colwin concludes with a benediction, exhorting us to muddle along with what we've got: "For every overworked professional woman of the nineties there was a depressed, bored, nonworking housewife of the fifties. We cannot go back in time. Instead, we must reinvent life for ourselves." We must find our own way.

And it's that nonchalant, enthusiastic, sometimes comforting, and above all realistic voice she writes in that imparts wisdom to me: that life is not a matter of following the rules and getting it all right, or even of roasting the lamb rump successfully. It is feeling your way forward step by step, one meal at a time, and knowing, as she puts it, that "a person cooking is a person giving: even the simplest food is a gift"—something Polly learned over simple lunches of bread and cheese. And even as we strive to do right and do good and love one another, we can learn from an imperfect meal, like stew in a pumpkin tureen, or an unexpected Christmas feast among strangers, that the best things in life may come when we can let down our guard for a moment and allow ourselves to simply be.

# FEAST
## LENTIL SOUP AND NO-KNEAD BREAD

No recipe for lamb rump here, since I am still working up the courage to try *that* again. Instead, let us turn to Laurie Colwin, who really, really loves lentils. Lentils appear in both of her books on cooking as a base for salads, a bed on which to serve other things, and, most notably, a foundation for good soup, which she talks about a *lot*. She has an entire chapter in *More Home Cooking* titled "Wonderful Lentil Soup." For Colwin, it's the ultimate comfort food.

And for me, a big pot of soup and a loaf of bread is the ideal large-group, low-budget meal. When I was in my mid-twenties, living in a 500-square-foot studio apartment with my husband, the 2008 recession hit. We were both still employed—me steadily in tech writing, him intermittently in film production—but many of our artist friends were struggling, and in an effort to do *something*, I hit upon the idea of hosting a monthly brunch in our tiny home to which all of our friends and their friends were invited. You didn't have to RSVP, and you didn't have to bring anything, though both were welcome.

This went on for a couple of years, during which we might have upwards of twenty-five people pile into our small place. Everyone sat on the floor—Laurie would have approved—and because there wasn't really anywhere to put a plate down, bowl-friendly food was ideal. I also never knew if the attendees would be vegetarian or dairy-free or have some other dietary restriction, and we couldn't afford to buy enormous quantities of more expensive foods, so I (like Laurie) figured out that lentils can stretch a very long way.

Those were some of the happiest days of our early marriage, and some of the most memorable. I don't have any of the precise recipes around that I used to use, and this isn't Colwin's exact recipe either. It's a version of what I made back in those days, and still make today, though if you come over for dinner I might take a stab at that lamb rump again.

## The Soup

1 sizable onion, or some shallots, peeled and chopped relatively small

2–4 cloves of garlic (you can never have too much garlic)

1–2 ribs of celery, chopped small

1–2 carrots, chopped small (just scrub, no need to peel)

1 c. lentils (green or French ones, probably; save the red ones, which get mushy and thick, for other splendid uses)

1 qt. water or any kind of broth, if you have it (I confess: I use bouillon a lot, as my freezer is too small to keep homemade broth around)

A glug of extra-virgin olive oil

Salt and pepper

A bay leaf, if you have one

1. Dump some oil into a pot—I use a ceramic-coated dutch oven—and heat it to medium-high. When the oil looks like it's glistening a little, add the onion and cook down, stirring often, till it's tender and becoming translucent; this usually takes about 5–6 minutes, but it can vary depending on your stovetop.

2. When the onions are almost ready, add the garlic and cook for another minute, stirring. Add carrots and celery. Salt and pepper them well, and cook for a few more minutes.

3. Then pour in the lentils, water or broth, and a bay leaf. Bring it to a boil, then let it simmer for about 30–40 minutes, till the lentils are at a texture you like. Ladle into bowls and serve with a swirl of olive oil on top.

But that's just a starting point for cocky, Colwin-approved improvisation. As she puts it, "In all your life you will be hard-pressed to find something as simple, soothing, and forgiving, as consoling as lentil soup. You can take things out of it or put things into it. It can be fancy or plain, and it will never let you down."

So here are some things you can add to lentil soup: chunks of potato; a little cumin; some thyme or any chopped fresh herb you can think of (with the possible exception of mint, though that might even work); cayenne pepper, dried red pepper flakes, or paprika for a bit of kick; green beans; chopped tomatoes from a can or tomato paste; kale or spinach, roughly chopped; a swirl of yogurt or croutons or both on top. Or anything else that seems good to you. If you mess it up, you'll just be learning a valuable lesson for next time, and honestly, you're probably the only person who will notice.

|||||||||||||||||||||||||||||||||

## No-Stress, No-Knead Bread

If you listen to Colwin's devotees discuss her bread chapter in *Home Cooking*, they often talk about how it didn't work for them. I grew up making bread, from flour we ground at home from whole grain, so the way dough should feel and what it should look like and smell like is hard-wired into me.

But a few years ago I discovered no-knead artisanal bread and I've never looked back. The traditional way of making bread requires a considerable head start, and I can't seem to plan for meals that far ahead. So I was delighted to discover there's a quicker way to make it.

I love this bread because it has four ingredients, if you don't count water. During the pandemic in 2020—the year in which I am writing this recipe—two of those ingredients suddenly became very scarce in grocery stores across the US: flour and yeast. I keep a big bag of King Arthur's white flour in my kitchen, as well as a cask of yeast in my freezer rather than those packets, which are kind of expensive. It's wonderful to be able to make fresh bread any time you want, but around April 2020, I became especially glad that I already had those ingredients on hand.

I've adapted this recipe from Mark Bittman, who knows a thing or two about simple home-cooked food.

---

3 c. flour (they will tell you bread flour, and if you've got it, great, but you can get away with other kinds of flour too)

1 packet of instant yeast, which comes out to 2 ¼ t. if you don't use the packets

1 ½ t. salt

Some olive oil

---

1. Put the flour, yeast, and salt in a big bowl with lots of extra space. Add 1 ½ cups warmish water and stir it all around. If you're accustomed to making bread, it will look completely wrong right now—all shaggy and floury. Do not fear! Help is on the way.

2. Cover the bowl with plastic wrap or something tight-fitting and leave it alone for four hours or so in a warm place. It will rise about double.

3. Smear oil onto your counter and turn the dough out onto it. (I usually make sure my hands are coated in oil to help this along.) You are not going to knead it! You simply need to fold it over on itself twice, then take the plastic wrap and cover it right there on the counter. Let it sit for 30 minutes.

4. While it's sitting, preheat your oven to 450 degrees, and put the vessel in which you intend to bake the bread into the oven so it can heat up too. I tend to use a deep cast-iron pan with a lid, or a dutch oven. You can use Pyrex or a casserole dish or whatever you have, as long as it's deep and has a lid.

5. When the dough is finished rising, pull the pan out of the oven and put it on the stovetop for a moment. Carefully pick up the dough with your hands and flip it into the pan, seam side up. It will sizzle just a little as the dough makes contact with the hot pan. With a potholder, grab the pan, and shake it once or twice to get the dough well-distributed.

6. Put the top on the pan and return it to the oven for 30 minutes. Then take the lid off and let it bake for an additional 15–30 minutes. (I usually err on the lower side, as I like to be able to bite through

the bread with ease, but crust enthusiasts may feel differently.) The crust will look beautifully browned. When you take it out, slide a fork or a spatula underneath the loaf to loosen it and turn it out onto a cooling rack. If you don't have a cooling rack—like me, a person who has never managed to remember to buy a cooling rack in her life—you can put it on a plate and it should be fine.

7. When it's cooled off a little, slice it up and serve it with room-temperature butter or cheese, and a bowl of delicious lentil soup.

# MORE SALT WITH LAURIE COLWIN

*Home Cooking* and *More Home Cooking*: The seminal texts for Colwin's food-loving readers, each chock-full of wonderful stories, recipes, and notes that are at times of questionable quality but always a delight to read.

*Happy All the Time*: One of Colwin's most famous and representative novels, focusing on two childhood friends who end up married to two young women and go through the various cheerful foibles of early married life.

*Family Happiness*: The novel about Polly, who must learn to give herself a break before she can grow.

*A Big Storm Knocked It Over*: The novel Colwin had just completed when she passed away, and which contains the marvelous passage about Christmas Eve in Vermont.

## CHAPTER THREE

# Agnès Varda

## Seeing Faces in the Scraps

In 2003, the filmmaker and artist Agnès Varda, who was then seventy-five years old, arrived at the Venice Biennale—perhaps the most prestigious art exhibition in the world—dressed as a potato.

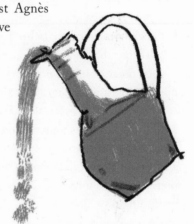

After decades as one of France's most venerated film-makers, or at least venerated by those in the know, Varda was at the Biennale to make her grand entry into the world of mixed-media visual art. She came with a three-screen video installation called *Patatutopia*, a play on words (typical of Varda): *patate* is French slang for potato—the proper term is *pomme de terre*, or earth-apple—and *utopia* is what you think it is. (One of the best reasons to learn even halting French as an English-speaking cinephile is to pick up on the puns and wordplay sprinkled liberally throughout Varda's films.)

When the viewer of *Patatutopia* enters the room, they are presented with an overwhelming quantity of potatoes—thirteen hundred pounds of them, in fact, arranged in a single layer on the floor of a white room. You can imagine the smell in that room: earthy, fresh, a bit like dirt. Above the *patates* towers the video triptych, each of the three screens featuring close-up, lovingly shot footage of heart-shaped potatoes in various stages of sprouting and shriveling. The potatoes experiencing an on-screen starring role were collected by Varda during the making of her celebrated 2000 documentary, *The Gleaners and I*.

Loving the anomalous heart formation of the spuds, Varda saved the potatoes for over two years, and she watched with curiosity and delight as their lives continued past the edible stage. If you've ever unearthed a potato from the back of a cabinet where it's accidentally fallen behind some stack of pasta boxes, you know what that looks like.

For most of us, a sprouting, wrinkly potato begs a wrinkled nose and a thud in the trash. But for Varda, it was an invitation to make art. And more than art, too; for Varda, the potato was a life lesson. It was a metaphor, because those overripe potatoes were not past their prime at all—they were simply moving into a new and productive phase. After all, the sprouts were a movement toward more life. The changing colors indicated all that was going on below the skin. And the heart shape became even more pronounced as the potato shrank into itself.

Years after the Biennale, in 2017, Varda would compare herself to the rangy spuds. "I see myself as a heart-shaped potato, growing again," she told a crowd in New York. She was referring to the trajectory of her film career, beginning with *La Pointe Courte*, which debuted in 1955. *La Pointe Courte* set the pace for the still-nascent French New Wave, the film movement that would change the way filmmakers all over the world thought about their own work in the future, a movement often associated with men like Jean-Luc Godard and François Truffaut. Varda spent much of her career being ignored by the critics who celebrated her male peers, even though she was ahead of them. And she kept innovating her whole life, even though investors were far more reticent to give her money than to fund her male counterparts. Always curious, always playful, Varda was undeterred.

A curious mix of highly self-conscious and frequently self-referential, she made work that was completely original. It would not be strictly accurate to say that Varda never seemed to care what people thought of her. In her later films, she reads notes received from both fans and detractors, and sometimes converses with them in person. She is interested in what they have to say, and why they say it, while remaining secure in her own opinions.

But then, this is a woman who showed up to the Biennale in a potato costume. Who made work following her own interests rather than commercial tastes for sixty-five years. Who was willing to forgo trends to forge her own. And boy, did she love potatoes.

||||||||||||||||||||||||||||||||

A free spirit from the start, Varda was born in Belgium in 1928, and back then was named Arlette. Her parents, a French woman and her Greek refugee husband, relocated when she was eleven to Sète, her mother's hometown on the Mediterranean. During World War II, they lived on a boat in the village. Eventually, the family moved to Paris.

At eighteen, she changed her name to Agnès, ran away for a summer, and worked briefly on a fishing boat before returning to Paris to attend the Sorbonne, where she studied psychology and literature. Even before she graduated, she started working as a photographer, a profession she'd return to over her lifetime. For a decade she was the official photographer for the Théâtre National Populaire, a leftist theater group in Paris.

Then she combined those interests and in 1954 made the film *La Pointe Courte*, set in a neighborhood of Sète. It mixed a stylized fiction story of a couple in the process of breaking up with documentary-style conversations between the village's fishermen. Well received when it played in theaters, it still had a limited release and for decades was difficult to see.

During this period, Varda moved to a small house situated on a courtyard on Paris's Rue Daguerre, in Montparnasse, on the southwest side of one of Paris's largest cemeteries. She would live there for the rest of her life. Within a few months of her daughter Rosalie's birth in 1958, she met the filmmaker Jacques Demy at a short film festival in Tours. They married in 1962, and Demy became Rosalie's adoptive father. In 1972 their son Mathieu was born. Both of Varda's children would be active participants in their mother's work, appearing in her films. And Rosalie helped support her aging mother during the making of her later work, eventually producing Varda's Oscar-nominated 2017 documentary, *Faces Places*, as well as her final film, *Varda by Agnès*, an essay film surveying Varda's vast oeuvre. It premiered in February 2019 at the Berlin Film Festival. Just a few weeks later, Varda passed away.

A trip through her filmography is eclectic and delightful, and also a semi-accidental guide to late twentieth-century politics. Varda was an outspoken feminist who signed manifestos and marched in the streets for women's rights in the 1960s and '70s; her films *Cléo from 5 to 7* (which anticipated Laura Mulvey's pioneering essay about the "male gaze" in cinema by more than a decade) and *One Sings, the Other Doesn't* (about female friendship and reproductive rights in France) are bedrocks of the feminist film canon.

In the late 1960s, Varda relocated with Demy to Los Angeles for a while. There she made *Black Panthers*, a documentary short about the Black Panther Party that gave an uncommon glimpse into the burgeoning movement, including interviews with the imprisoned Huey P. Newton, one of the party's cofounders.

Then came her wild tragicomical 1969 film, *Lions Love (. . . and Lies)*, starring Warhol muse Viva, along with the lyricists and lead performers from *Hair*, in an exploration of the brain-bending combination of free love, malaise, and terror that marked late-1960s Hollywood. Her movies always revealed an insatiably curious mind. She leaned into seeing—*really* seeing—the world as it was, or could be.

And her subjects felt seen, and loved, by Varda. Her 2017 film, *Faces Places*, which came near the end of her life, richly illustrates this. She collaborated with the thirty-five-year-old street artist JR for the film; his work often consists of pasting large-scale black-and-white photographic images in public spaces. In the movie, they travel to villages around France, talking to locals, hearing their stories, taking their pictures, and printing them in a van, their mobile studio. The prints are massive, and they paste them on the sides of buildings, shipping crates, walls, and even an old bunker, which once belonged to the Nazis, that has tumbled off a seaside cliff and now perches on the beach. The pair's unlikely friendship grows as the film progresses.

*Faces Places* captures all kinds of people all over rural France, but the film is primarily about how we see one another's faces. Throughout the movie, Varda ribs JR about his signature sunglasses, which he refuses to take off; in this way, he reminds her of her old friend Jean-Luc Godard, who sports a similar affectation but once took off his glasses to star in a short film Varda directed in 1961. (It later appeared as a film-within-a-film in *Cléo from 5 to 7*.) At the climax of the film, she takes JR to meet Godard, but Godard stands her up, reducing Varda to tears. Trying to comfort her, JR agrees to let her see his face, but Varda's eyesight is waning, so when he takes off his shades, all she can see is a blur. The film ends with the pair sitting companionably on a bench, gazing out at the ocean together.

Seeing people is what she always wanted to do, to see and to document. "I never wanted to say anything," she told an interviewer late in her life. "I just wanted to look at people and share."

||||||||||||||||||||||||||||

But not only people. Potatoes, too. It makes sense that Varda's *patate*-philia came through her love of watching people. In 2000, forty years into her career, she made a film titled *Les glaneurs et la glaneuse* (*The Gleaners and I*, for Anglophone audiences). As in many of her documentaries, she does the narration. In the film's early moments, Varda explains that she started to notice the bending and stooping posture of "gleaners," people who bend over to pick up discarded items on the street—food, clothing, knickknacks, whatever they can save from the trash.

Varda had long been in the habit of watching people on the street, thinking about them, and *seeing* them. In 1958, with *La Pointe Courte* under her belt but little funding to make another feature-length film, she made several short films instead. Among them was a short called *L'Opéra Mouffe* (in English titled *Diary of a Pregnant Woman*), a favorite of mine. Varda was pregnant with Rosalie at the time and living on the Rue Mouffetard, which today is a beloved street full of shops and restaurants that attracts both locals and tourists, but back then was a bit more sordid and run down.

In the film, Varda intersperses images of shops and shoppers with drunks and derelicts and, perhaps surprisingly, close-ups of naked bodies, those of a pregnant woman and of a man and woman in love. The curves, dips, and textures of bodies mix together with the almost palpable smells and sights of the storefronts and food in the stalls. An opera, if you will.

She'd later say it was her favorite of her early films. "I enjoyed capturing in the middle of the Mouffetard markets the confusion between a stomach heavy with child and one of food," Varda told an interviewer in 1965. (Sometimes her English needs a little extra parsing.)

"And so many contradictions!" she continued. "A pregnant woman watches the waves of people, especially older people, on a steep incline and she thinks: 'They were all newborns once; someone sprinkled fresh talcum powder on them and then kissed their little behinds.' That's the kind of thought that pushes our gaze to the fine line that separates cruelty from tenderness."

Varda often spoke in interviews over the years of this revelation she had as a young, pregnant woman—that every person you see was once a baby, beloved by someone, helpless and in need of a diaper change. The stories we carry around with us mattered to her. "What interests me is precisely the silent, secret, inexpressible things that are in people. There are as many things in the domain of the instincts as in the domain of feelings," she said in another interview.

The Rue Mouffetard of *L'Opéra Mouffe* is different from the one I've strolled down a dozen times in recent years. After a few long sojourns in Paris, the city feels like my second home, the place I'm most comfortable in the world that isn't New York. So whenever I'm in Europe for work, I always make a point of returning home through Paris. I usually stay in Montparnasse. Both Rue Mouffetard and Varda's eventual home on Rue Daguerre are within a stone's throw of the flat where I usually stay, and both are market streets.

Rue Mouffetard hasn't been paved over, so it's still cobblestone, and walking down the street, you can buy some of the finest cheese, seafood, wine, vegetables, and, especially, rotisserie chickens with the accompanying roasted potatoes, which have cooked to creamy perfection in the fat dripping from the slowly spinning chickens. It's extraordinary, and it's impossible to smell without wanting some immediately. *L'Opéra Mouffe* shows a less

Instagram-ready version of the street, but as with many streets in Paris, it's still recognizable well over half a century later.

Nearly two decades after *L'Opera Mouffe*, Varda echoed the short in another project—a documentary about the shop-keepers on her new street, Rue Daguerre. Now with a toddler running around her home, she couldn't roam very far. So she plugged in her camera to an electrical outlet, and with a ninety-meter power cable, she took to the street. She named the film *Daguerrotypes*, for the early photographic process, and created small, moving portraits of her neighbors: the baker and his wife, the man who fixes clocks, the butcher, the accordion store owner, and other shop owners, like the couple who owns The Blue Thistle.

"It's my neighborhood," she told an interviewer. "These are my shops and I've always been interested in them. Especially one of them, The Blue Thistle, a sort of dressmaker's, bazaar, and perfume shop all in one. It's the only place I know where you can get twenty grams of rice-powder or thirty centiliters of eau de Cologne."

Varda imbues the film with a magic that comes from just watching ordinary people at work. The baker's wife takes orders for baguettes and makes change. The baker weighs dough, shapes it, and slides it into the giant oven. The butcher slices steaks and pork chops for customers. The grocer explains to a woman, with immense patience, that he doesn't have any canned full-fat milk; he only has sterilized full-fat milk in bottles or canned skim milk. We listen to Varda ask the shopkeepers about where they were born, how they met their spouses, what they dream about. And while they're shy at first, it's clear they're proud of their work.

It's a mesmerizing portrait of a neighborhood, and it makes me think of the wine shop, the cheese and pâté shop, the fish-monger, and the boulangerie where I get my daily bread when

I'm in Paris. The courteous dance of *bonjour* and *merci* and *au revoir* that you learn to interact with shopkeepers there—a far more polite experience than I have shopping at home. And the delight of weak ties, of interacting with acquaintances—the same cheesemonger, the same waiter, the same wine store owner each time I go in, something distinctly Parisian that I miss when I'm "home" far more than I ever expected.

I suspect Varda always harbored fond feelings for the humble potato, a splendid staple in butter-rich French cooking. But when she was making her 2000 film, *The Gleaners and I*, she took that love to a whole new level.

In the film, Varda trains her camera on people in both the city and the countryside who gather the discards of others. Varda became interested, she said, in "who eats my leftovers," and was arrested by the bearing of the gleaners, the hunched, humbling posture of rummaging through what's on the street. They reminded her of Jean-François Millet's painting *Les Glaneuses* (*The Gleaners*), in which women stoop to gather the leftovers from an already-harvested wheat field.

But as the film progresses, her perspective on gleaning expands, and so does ours. Some of the gleaners, of course, collect discards and leftovers because they are poor. But others are primarily concerned with waste. In one place, she discovers that after the potato harvest, the potatoes that are rejected because they're too big or too small or too misshapen to sell get dumped in a field, forming small mountains. Those in the know can come pick through the mounds and collect buckets full to carry home or bring to a food bank. And that field is where Varda discovers her beloved heart-shaped potatoes, which she takes home to observe.

She also talks with gleaners who glean all kinds of stuff. There are those who practice what Americans call "dumpster diving," rescuing food discarded by grocers for passing its sell-by date but perfectly fine to eat. She talks to people who harvest oysters that have washed out of oyster farms and onto the public beach, as well as to the oyster farmers who watch tolerantly when the gleaners technically cross their property line. Others collect olives left on the branches after the harvest, or grapes that are discarded by wineries in order to ensure their wines' "reserve" status. All of the gleaners have different reasons for gleaning, but listening to Varda talk with them changes the act of gleaning into participation in a noble fight against the tyrannies of overweening capitalism.

Watching *The Gleaners and I*, I was reminded of the staggering statistics I'd read about wasted food in the US. Americans throw away eighty billion pounds of food every year, roughly 30 to 40 percent of the domestic food supply. That's almost 219 pounds per person, and it's even more shocking when you consider that about thirty-seven million Americans live in a state of food insecurity. Among the reasons that people use to "excuse" this profound waste is that Americans rely on expiration labels, rather than trusting tongue or nose to determine if our food has gone bad. Many of us are so far removed from the food production process that we're not able to intuitively tell if food is still edible or if it bears food-borne illness. I'm as guilty of this as anyone; I have a visceral response of vague nausea when I think about eating meat that was "best by" yesterday or food rescued from a dumpster, even if it's still in the packaging.

But my Paris stints do help me see another way of living, one more attuned to "daily" bread. On my first visit, I quickly realized that you can't buy that staple of French kitchens, the delightful baguette, too far in advance, as it turns hard by the next day. (This gets tricky when many boulangeries are closed on Sundays.) So daily baguette shopping becomes essential, and for many Parisians—who frequently have tiny refrigerators and few places to store extra food—that means daily food shopping, too. A walk home from work includes passing each of your neighborhood food vendors: the fishmonger, the patisserie, the fromagerie, the grocery. You can, if you wish, easily pick up all the ingredients for dinner each night on your way home.

Living in New York City, I could almost do the same thing. I pass several bodegas (the Spanish word New Yorkers use for their corner grocery) on my commute, plus a fish market, a bakery, and my neighborhood wine store. But New Yorkers are all about optimization, so more often I place a grocery order online at the start of the week, and then find, by the weekend, that I haven't quite used up the mixed greens before they go mushy, or that I overcalculated how quickly I'd get to those chicken thighs. A freezer helps, but it doesn't solve the issue. My shelves and cabinets are still full of foods with a long shelf life, bought at the start of the pandemic. I have the immense privilege to have more food than I need, to let my eyes grow bigger than my stomach.

*The Gleaners and I* is a call to change my ways. Among the things I've tried to implement is buying less and trusting that the groceries I have will last the week or that I can find a way to stretch them. Or I order vegetables from one of the companies that's recently sprung up in the US expressly to rescue "ugly" produce and get it to customers to cut down on food waste (though I'm still waiting for a heart-shaped potato).

The last person featured in Varda's film is a man named Alain. He occupies the end of the film, I think because he embodies, for her, the contradictions and glories you unearth when you slow down to listen to a stranger. Talking with him, Varda discovers he has a master's degree, sells newspapers on the street, and lives in public housing mostly occupied by immigrants; there, he teaches French classes free of charge, an entirely volunteer task.

Early in the morning, he gets on the train from the suburbs to gather vegetables and fruits that Paris's open-air market vendors leave behind. Like all of her favorite subjects, he defies everyone's expectations. Two years later, Varda revisits Alain in a follow-up film, and he's getting ready to run the Paris marathon—with running shoes he gleaned, of course.

Throughout the film, her conversations with Alain and the other gleaners are mixed with Varda's reflections on her own aging and her filmmaking practice of nearly fifty years. Now a widow (Demy died in 1990), she contemplates her life and work, the odd beauty of hands growing wrinkled and spotted with age. She starts to talk about her artistic practice as "gleaning," too.

Listening to her talk about her own gleaning in this way snapped something into place for me about her work as a filmmaker. Varda has always shown genuine interest in the people who normally fall outside of the camera's frame. For her, filmmaking is "gleaning ideas, images, and emotions," she told an interviewer. "It's like gleaning first impressions. I allow myself to live in the film, to 'let in' the film, because I thought by making a film like [Gleaners] I don't want to be separate from it, to live in another world than those who speak so honestly, so clearly about themselves, and speak about situations in which they could be ashamed or wish to hide or wish to say 'don't bother with me.'"

The way Varda made art from the beginning of her career was always with a gleaner's eye. There's a pure transparency, a kindness, an originality to her work that can be attributed to her lifelong practice of simply paying attention to whatever her peers were ignoring at the time, whether gleaners and potatoes or the streets in her neighborhood, full of people who once were tiny newborns. "Filming, especially a documentary, is gleaning," she said in 2009. "Because you pick what you find; you bend; you go around; you are curious; you try to find out where are things."

She went on to note that the analogy can't be pushed too far, because "we don't just film the leftovers." But in her later films, she often held up for the camera the souvenirs she purchased, the odd bits and pieces she picked up around the world, and the items she saved and treasured that people had sent her, particularly after seeing *The Gleaners and I*. The things of the world meant something to her not so much for their functionality or their use, but for themselves.

And she may have picked this up early on. In 1970, reflecting on her time at the Sorbonne studying with the philosopher Gaston Bachelard, Varda said that he "really blew my mind. . . . He taught us to study writers not only by the stories they told but by the material things they mentioned." You can learn a lot by the material things Varda mentions, and shows, and lingers on, and urges us to truly see.

All of this brings me back to Varda, dressed as a potato, at her Venice Biennale opening, and how she carted that costume to art shows around the world for years, many of them also centered on potatoes. (People started calling her "Dame Patate.") It's the kind of playful move that brings down the guard rails that people set up for themselves in "high art" settings. You can't be too snobby about art when the artist is wandering around dressed like a potato—dirty even when you scrub it, unremarkable, lumpy, prone to shrivel and sprout. Varda's love of the heart-shaped potato and the path it takes when it's past its edible stage speaks of a sensibility that revels in forgotten and discarded things. The people and stories that don't make it onto camera. The film that only screens for a few people. The shopkeeper who trims fat from pork loins and sells cans of skim milk to old women and teaches the neighborhood kids to play accordion. The man crumpled on the corner who used to be a baby, someone's baby. And she trusts her audience to be interested, too.

That's not every filmmaker's position, let alone every artist's. Too often filmmakers, rather than serving up a complex and sumptuous feast, dish out something easily digested, something that can't be taken the wrong way and doesn't require much in the way of chewing. Varda considered her audience differently—she thought of them, of us, as people with stories, capable of looking at one another just the way she did. "Ultimately, I believe that people have a taste for reflection," Varda said to an interviewer in 1967. "They have a taste that leads them to reflection. I often think of my public as a mass of people whom I really like, but just because we have a friendly relationship doesn't mean that we can't talk seriously or lightheartedly about important subjects. It's really on the level of feeling that this connection interests me."

And she thought of her work as a kind of table around which her audience would be able to gather. "I believe that ultimately people have a lot in common but that they don't have a lot of opportunities to think about this or act on it," she said. "So I want my films to act as revelations. This is what interests me. There are questions that I personally find intensely interesting and which I'd like to find answers to. I try to ask these questions with enough clarity and enough ambiguity to get my viewers to ask for themselves."

When Varda passed away in 2019, having become something of a style icon and a celebrity following *The Gleaners and I* and, especially, the Oscar nomination for *Faces Places*, she was still living on Rue Daguerre. As usual, fans and film lovers felt the need to pay homage to her. And they did so in the way they knew she'd love best. On Varda's doorstep, in front of the pink atelier where she lived and worked and loved, a tribute to the artist grew: a pile of heart-shaped potatoes.

# FEAST
## ROASTED CHICKEN AND POTATOES

One of the most memorable meals I have ever eaten in Paris was a particularly superb *poulet roti*, French-style rotisserie chicken and potatoes. You can buy it most anywhere, in a grocery store, on a market street, but someone sent my husband and me to Rue Mouffetard for what they claimed was the best around.

We never found that restaurant, but in hungry desperation, we located another shop with rotisserie chickens spinning slowly in the window—you can hardly miss them—and laid down our euros. The thing about *poulet roti* is the process by which they make it: rotisserie roasting gets the skin of the chicken good and crisp, and small potatoes cook nestled into trays beneath the rotating chickens, which means they roast in the chicken fat. It is sumptuous, even if some consider it essentially fast food. (Also, a lot of butter is involved, and you honestly haven't had butter until you've had French butter.)

It is not easy to replicate an actual rotisserie at home unless you have a lot of time, money, and counter space. But it is possible to evoke a *poulet roti*, which has the key ingredient: potatoes. And as a bonus, this will work with any kind of potato, no matter how small or misshapen it might be. Go to the market and buy them loose, and feel free to pick out the oddest-looking little potatoes you can find. If you're lucky, maybe you'll even find some heart-shaped ones.

I don't know where I got this recipe—probably cobbled together from various recipes over the years—but it's the way to go.

---

1 whole chicken, about 3 lb.

Around 3 c. small potatoes. If you want to (gasp) not use
    potatoes, or if you don't have enough, most any root

vegetable will do: carrots, parsnips, or whatever was at the market; if they're large, cut them up so the pieces are around an inch square.

½ c. unsalted butter (one stick) at room temperature—it should be soft

2 onions, cut into thick slices

1 lemon (I have also used an orange in a pinch)

4–6 cloves of garlic, unpeeled and smashed

Fresh thyme, about 8–12 sprigs' worth

Dried thyme or Herbes de Provence

Olive oil

Salt (the flakier, the better)

Pepper

---

1. Preheat your oven to 425 degrees, chop your vegetables, and get out a roasting pan.

2. Pat the chicken dry, especially the cavity, and put it on a plate.

3. Put the vegetables in the roasting pan. Drizzle olive oil onto them (several tablespoons' worth) and zest the lemon over them. Add 6–8 sprigs of fresh thyme, plus salt and pepper, and mix it around. This works best with your hands. Make sure the vegetables are well coated.

4. Carefully place the chicken directly on top of the vegetables, almost as if they're propping it up, so it doesn't touch the pan.

5. Poke the lemon a couple of times with a fork and stick it inside the chicken. Push a few more sprigs of thyme and 2–4 cloves of garlic inside the chicken too. (In my opinion, you can never have enough garlic, though French cooking goes light on it, so do whatever you want.)

6. Take about a quarter of the room-temperature butter and cut it into small pieces. Slip them under the skin of the chicken; you may need to use your fingers to separate the skin from the meat in order to do this.

7. Take another quarter of the room-temperature butter and, with your fingers, spread it on the outside of the skin of the bird. Pepper it, and sprinkle with dried thyme or Herbes de Provence. (I have also used paprika for a fun alternative when I'm looking to spice things up.)

8. Place the whole tray into the oven for 20 minutes; the skin will start to brown.

9. On the stovetop, melt the remaining butter (¼ or ½ a stick) with the remaining garlic. Just melt it; don't let it boil. This is your bird-basting butter.

10. After the chicken has browned for 20 minutes, turn the oven down to 400 degrees. You're going to roast it for about 60–75 minutes more—this will depend a bit on the size of your chicken—and baste it every 20 minutes with the garlicky butter. You can roughly calculate the total roasting time at 20 minutes per pound, but a meat thermometer is your best bet. One year my husband got me

the world's best meat thermometer for Christmas, and I'm pretty sure the rest of my family was scandalized by the utilitarian, humdrum gift, but it's honestly the best present I've ever gotten, I think? Anyhow, you'll know it's done when you stick a meat thermometer into the thigh and it registers 165 degrees.

11. As noted, every 20 minutes you'll want to baste the bird with the butter from your stovetop. This is most easily accomplished with a baster, which you can use to suck up some of the butter and then apply it to the chicken. I have also, in the absence of a baster, used a silicone brush, or simply a spoon or ladle, with care.

12. When the chicken is done, take the pan out of the oven and place the chicken on a platter, a large cutting board with grooves to catch the juices, or a big plate of some kind. Stir the vegetables and put them back in the oven for a few minutes more; keep an eye on them till they look like they're the level of crispiness you want them to be. (They'll be very soft and buttery!)

13. Tent some foil over the chicken and let it sit for 10 minutes. Then remove the foil and carve it up. Bon appetit.

This is super, super tasty, and here's a bonus: you can use the carcass to make broth afterward. (You can even put it in last chapter's lentil soup.) Don't waste the leftovers. Agnès would not be pleased.

# MORE SALT WITH AGNÈS VARDA

*The Complete Films of Agnès Varda*, from the Criterion Collection: This is the motherlode, the gold standard. It consists of fifteen discs, each containing a thematic "program," from "Married Life" to "No Shelter" to "Here and There." The special features include introductions to many of the films by Varda herself, explorations of her work, behind-the-scenes featurettes, more short films Varda made for TV, and a wealth of other materials.

The Criterion set also includes a 200-page booklet with essays, introductions, and critical appraisals by prominent film critics and historians, along with photographs she took and images from her art installations.

*Agnès Varda: Interviews*, edited by T. Jefferson Kline: A book laying out decades of interviews that Varda did throughout her career, tracing the way her work, themes, and thought evolved.

ELLa BaKER

## CHAPTER FOUR

# ELLA BAKER

## HAMBURGERS, WHISKEY, AND RADICAL HOSPITALITY

On Easter weekend in April 1960, something was afoot in Raleigh, North Carolina. One hundred twenty-six student delegates from all over the country arrived on the campus of Shaw University, a historically Black institution. The delegates represented colleges in the north, fifty-eight sit-in protests occurring in twelve different states, and a number of student groups including Students for a Democratic Society and the Southern Christian Leadership Conference (SCLC), the organization presided over by Dr. Martin Luther King. The students had been invited to Raleigh by King. But the conference they were about to attend was all Ella Baker's doing.

Baker was in her fifties and a seasoned organizer in the Civil Rights Movement. The month of the conference marked two and a half often-frustrating years she had spent as the interim director of the SCLC. In her time with the organization, she was very effective—nobody organized and mobilized like Miss Ella Jo Baker—but she frequently found herself in conflict with King, whom she viewed with some suspicion for what she saw as privileging charisma over getting his hands dirty on the ground. What's more, the organization's dynamics and decisions were heavily weighted toward its male leaders; Baker might have been running the organization, but she knew she'd never be instated as its permanent director, which the SCLC's leadership saw as a job for a man.

But as she'd been working, she'd also been watching the headlines. Just a couple of months earlier, four Black freshmen at the North Carolina Agricultural and Technical State University (A&T)—inspired by King's philosophy of nonviolence—had decided to tackle segregation in their town of Greensboro head-on. On Monday, February 1, 1960, Joseph McNeil, Franklin McCain, Ezell Blair Jr., and David Richmond went to the Woolworth's at 132 South Elm Street and sat down at the stainless steel lunch counter, which had sixty-six seats. Each asked for a cup of coffee. They were heckled by customers and refused service by the waitress. The store manager asked them to leave, but they stayed put. They remained till the store closed.

On Tuesday, more than twenty students showed up at Woolworth's, this time with homework to keep them occupied. On Wednesday, over sixty people turned up. On Thursday, they numbered three hundred, still mostly students. On Friday, several hundred protesters showed up again, and were confronted by a group of fifty white men who tried to keep them out. By Saturday, after a rally on the A&T campus, over a thousand people tried to cram into Woolworth's.

The movement began to spread. Students in cities like Nashville, Jackson, Raleigh, Richmond, and many more staged their own sit-ins at lunch counters. Eventually sit-ins would occur in one hundred cities both across the South and into the North. Sometimes the students were attacked. The movement spread from lunch counters to libraries, pools, beaches, and other public spaces. In response, the City of Greensboro adopted more stringent segregation policies and arrested forty-five students; the students struck back by launching boycotts of all segregated lunch counters. Those counters lost a third of their customers—and money, as always, talks. In the end, Woolworth's desegregated all of its lunch counters across the country.

From her position at the SCLC, Baker watched what was happening, filled with the conviction that these students had an energy that could accomplish something even more profound. They were brave, and bold, and unshakable. And they were insisting on something both simple and radical: they had the right to be treated like human beings, in the same spaces as their white neighbors.

Baker had worked at the highest levels of influential activist organizations for her whole career, including at the NAACP. She held the unwavering belief that the key to lasting change didn't lie with charismatic leaders or national organizations. Instead, she believed that the power was present in ordinary people to guide themselves and the nation toward change. "Baker's unfaltering confidence in the common people was the bedrock of her political vision," her biographer, Barbara Ransby, writes. "It was with them that she felt the locus of power should reside."

The students' efforts were largely grassroots and decentralized; they inspired one another, and yet they operated separately from one another. They were spurred by the kind of nonviolence advocated by King and the SCLC, and yet they were far from nonconfrontational. They were young and energetic. And Baker wanted to support them.

So she organized the conference in Raleigh and, knowing that the students looked up to King, asked him to send the invitation. She coaxed the $800 needed to put together such an event from the SCLC budget and lined up King as the opening speaker. They called the event the Southern Leadership Conference.

King kicked things off, but it's Baker's speech that people still talk about. The talk itself wasn't recorded, but after the conference Baker wrote an article that summarized her address, and it was published in the activist newspaper *The Southern Patriot*. "The Southern Leadership Conference made it crystal clear that current sit-ins and other demonstrations are concerned with something much bigger than a hamburger or even a giant-sized Coke," she wrote, echoing what she'd said to the students. "Whatever may be the difference in approach to their goal, the Negro and white students, North and South, are seeking to rid America of the scourge of racial segregation and discrimination—not only at lunch counters, but in every aspect of life."

This movement was partly about the right to have a cup of coffee in peace, to order a hamburger without rejection. But it wasn't just about a burger, a coffee, a Coke. It was about everything.

Baker knew about the fundamental importance of bringing the fight for justice to the places where people eat. Decades earlier, while traveling by train as part of her work with the NAACP, she regularly confronted Jim Crow policies in dining cars. In one instance, in May 1943, she was traveling on a first-class ticket between Miami and New York City, and she wanted lunch. She sat at a dining table that, according to Florida law, should have been available to Black passengers. But the steward asked her to leave.

A cornerstone of Baker's beliefs was that in order to end Jim Crow, she and others must live their lives *as if* segregationist policies were unlawful. Behaving as though requiring Black Americans to live as second-class citizens was unacceptable would shock people into realizing that it was, in fact, unacceptable.

Modeling a better world, insisting on its possibility, could help bring that world into being.

So when the dining car steward asked Baker to leave her seat, she refused. Two military policemen arrived and began to physically remove her from the seat; one bruised her leg. Baker did what she thought was best: she shouted to the others in the dining car, "This man is overstepping his authority!" And the military police let go of her.

Later that day, the train's conductor located Baker in her seat and told her that it was unlawful for whites and "colored" folks to eat in the same restaurant in Florida. But Baker informed him that it was also against the law to not provide dining accommodations for first-class passengers. The conductor refused to apologize even as he served her dinner in her seat. Baker later filed a complaint with the railroad.

For Baker, experiences like this reaffirmed that insisting on being seated and served wasn't just about getting lunch. It was about building a more just world.

The importance of helping others was drummed into Baker from the start. Like Edna Lewis's grandparents, Baker's grandmother, Josephine Elizabeth "Bet" Baker, was born into slavery, the daughter of an enslaved woman and her white enslaver, whose jealous wife murdered Bet's mother with poison.

Baker grew up hearing her grandmother Bet's harrowing stories, which seemed far from her own life. Born in 1903 in Norfolk, Virginia, Baker enjoyed a comfortable middle-class life with her family. She told one interviewer that her family was "never hungry. They could share their food with people. So, you shared your lives with people." Baker's parents and grandparents were benevolent members of their community, but there was what Ransby, Baker's biographer, calls a kind of "elitism" baked into their Christian charity. "Implicit in this philosophy is the idea that the disadvantaged are not fully capable of helping them-selves," Ransby writes. A constant subtext was that the more fortunate must show the poor what needs fixing and how they ought to fix it.

Baker came to reject this notion wholeheartedly and spent her life working from the exact opposite assumption—that yes, it's the duty of more privileged people to come to the aid of the poor and oppressed, but also that those they want to help should be given space and support to determine what they need to do and to speak out on their own behalf, rather than having some-one speak for them. She railed against paternalism. "She came to see what she described as the hidden strength within people and communities that on the surface appeared to be without resources or recourse," Ransby notes.

This is why Baker saw the struggle for freedom as "radical." Demanding freedom in the face of opposition and oppression is, of course, always radical, in the sense that it's new and different and many people consider it extreme. But Baker was clear that she meant the word *radical* in its other sense: having to do with the *root* of things, their essence, their foundation. Radical activ-ism goes to the root, to the communities that have need, and gives them the resources and space they need to assess their own needs, speak up on their own behalf, and fight their own battles. "Baker's unfaltering confidence in the common people was the bedrock of her political vision," Ransby observes. "It was with them that she felt the locus of power should reside."

Baker's perspective represented one of two major ways of organizing that arose in the modern fight against Black oppres-sion. Her method was to empower communities. The other was driven more by large-scale events and recognizable faces, a model employed by figures like King. The two methods worked in parallel and sometimes chafed against one another. But that meant Baker was as key a figure in the fight for civil rights as King. (The contemporary Black Lives Matter movement, which is decentralized, locally based, and community-driven, finds its own roots in Baker's paradigm.)

The white activist Anne Braden, a close friend of Baker's, said that one of the things she learned in her early activist work was that the best advocates for the rights of poor Black people were not middle-class white and Black people; the best advocates were the poor Black people themselves. "This is a concept that southern segregationists and the FBI found difficult to grasp," Ransby notes. "They persisted in the erroneous assumption that southern Blacks would simply not stand up for themselves and demand fair treatment unless someone 'smarter'—white or northern—put them up to it."

Baker rejected that kind of arrogance wholesale. In Baker's framework, organizing is decentralized, centered in individual communities. The role of an outside facilitator is to guide, listen, provide resources, and create spaces in which conversations can happen. But the setting of priorities and the actual advocacy is best done by the ordinary people in those communities, not an interloper.

What that means, practically, is two things. One is that someone like Baker—who moved to New York City following her graduation from Shaw and spent a great deal of her early career traveling the South for her work with the NAACP—was mainly there to listen. And the other is that a whole lot of talking had to happen. Those conversations would happen in the everyday places where people gathered. Barber shops. Churches. Public spaces. And, of course, in people's homes, and most of all around people's tables.

"In her travels throughout the South on behalf of the NAACP," Ransby writes, "she met hundreds of ordinary black people and established enduring relationships with many of them. She slept in these people's homes, ate at their tables, spoke in their churches, and earned their trust. And she was never too busy, despite her intense schedule, to send off a batch of personal thank-you notes, sending regards to those she did not contact directly and expressing gratitude for the support and hospitality she had received."

Not much of a cook herself, Baker was constantly on the road and wholly focused on the work. Yes, she knew how to cook—her mother would have made sure of that—and was famous for her lamb stew. But she didn't keep much food at her apartment in Harlem and more often found herself eating at the tables of others, listening to them, hearing what they were thinking and needing.

That doesn't mean she wasn't appreciative of the value and purpose of a good meal, or a gathering that centered on food. After all, she was a Southern girl, and she spent much of her time in the South, where food is at the center of any gathering. Discussion and dining, dialogue and whiskey were inseparable. Patricia Parker, an activist-scholar who works today in the tradition of Baker, highlights that relationship in her book on Baker's "catalytic leadership":

> When I write grants to support social justice leadership work, they always include a hefty food budget, because I know that [as in Baker's leadership work] much of our time will be spent in gatherings to create and sustain our work as we make new connections and strengthen existing ones. . . . Community-building leadership is, centrally, about convening: people gather to create experiences, to connect, and to value that connectedness as human beings. Convening spaces of fellowship in which community experts and academic

as well as other sources of expertise can connect is vital
to orienting a collective toward its work.

An early space of fellowship that shaped Baker, Parker notes,
was the home of George and Josephine Schuyler. George was a
Black author and a famous journalist, and Josephine, his wife,
was white—a marriage that at the time would have been illegal in some parts of the country and highly unusual everywhere.
Josephine had to conceal her marriage, as well as the birth of
their daughter, Philippa, from her Texan family.

The Schuylers lived in Harlem. In the 1930s, a mutual friend
introduced George Schuyler and Baker, who was working with
grassroots activist groups, and he became a kind of mentor to her.
(Later in life, Schuyler's politics would swing far to the right.)
The Schuylers' home was large and spacious and very comfortable, and on many evenings they would gather their friends for a
kind of salon, with elegant food, libations, and of course lots of
discussion. You didn't need an invitation; the door was open to
anyone who wanted to come. It was "a site for an animated discourse that helped define African-American public life," Ransby
writes. "In these venues, politics and culture were debated and
areas of consensus were formed and reformed. The activists,
writers, and artists who convened regularly at the Schuylers'
apartment had a certain romantic appeal about them. They were
young, creative, bold, witty, and cosmopolitan."

Baker loved the gatherings, less for who she might brush
shoulders with in the latter years of the Harlem Renaissance
and more for the mutual sharpening of ideas, with conversations
that might last till dawn. Like many people across history, she
found encouragement and challenge, inspiration and friendship
in those salons.

That experience—and many others around kitchen tables and
in Harlem's diners and restaurants in her early years—shaped

how Baker connected with and saw other people. She believed in creating "free spaces," moments and places where people could gather and talk with one another without fear of being criticized if they questioned established norms or things that seemed obvious. Those free spaces already often existed in the very places Baker visited as an organizer—theaters and arts centers, hair salons, cultural institutions, church potlucks, dinner tables. And free spaces could also be created and grown, in deliberately arranged meetings and gatherings. They were where people could tell their own stories.

Baker was *fascinated* by stories. A friend and fellow organizer, Bob Moses, recalled being with Baker on the streets of Harlem, where Baker lived. He said she would stop total strangers and ask, "Hello, brother. And where do you hail from?" Those who knew her testified to her abiding interest in everyone she met. Not only did she believe that individual people's stories were worthy of her attention, but she believed this in a radical, foundational way—and rebuked those who thought otherwise.

It's part of why she was so frustrated with the SCLC, which was led by ministers who, in Baker's view, were accustomed to only seeing women in domestic roles. "They were most comfortable talking to women about 'how well they cooked, and how beautiful they looked,' she complained," according to Ransby. "Baker's deliberate avoidance of conventional femininity made a number of her male clerical colleagues rather uneasy." Baker didn't dress to be a "fashion plate" and rarely spoke about her own marriage (to her college sweetheart, Bob Roberts, until they divorced in 1958). And it's probably no accident that she stayed mostly out of her own kitchen. Challenging chauvinism was as much a part of trying to live the freedom she wished to see in the world as any of the rest of it, and the kitchen could be a historically fraught place for any woman, let alone one descended from enslaved women who cooked for white people. Baker wished to educate by example.

But as much as she protected her own privacy, Baker loved hearing other people's stories, whether they were young students or had grandkids of their own, and whether she knew them before their conversation or not. She would go out of her way to hear them.

In 1962, Dorothy Dawson, a young white civil rights worker, was passing through Baker's offices in Atlanta when she learned that a young man named Raymond Johnson had died in Monroe, Alabama, in a suspicious drowning that authorities were calling an accident. Dawson decided to drive there for the funeral and to visit Raymond's mother, Azalea Johnson, whom Dawson knew but Baker had never met. Baker asked to come along, in part to get an on-the-ground sense of the climate in Monroe, and in part to spend time with Johnson, who was a leader of the movement in Monroe. They didn't make it in time for the funeral, but Baker and Dawson stayed with Johnson for several days. Later, Dawson recalled that the three women spent most of their time at Johnson's table, eating and drinking Jim Beam bourbon, talking about Southern politics, and telling the story of Raymond's life.

What they modeled in their whiskey-laced visit was the power that sharing stories can have to build a connection between guest and host and create space for change. Priya Basil, author of *Be My Guest: Reflections on Food, Community, and the Meaning of Generosity*, explains that sharing stories fosters its own kind of host-guest relationship that goes two ways:

> Stories enact a form of mutual hospitality. What is a story if not an enticement to stay? You're invited in, but right away you must reciprocate and host the story back, through concentration: whether you read

or hear a narrative—from a book or a person—you need to listen to really understand. Granting complete attention is like giving a silent ovation. Story and listener open, unfold into and harbor each other.

There is, Basil later writes, an "equalizing potential" in breaking bread with strangers—a potential Baker lived into fully.

When Baker wrote her article summarizing her speech at the Southern Leadership Conference, she reiterated that the issue the sit-in movement was confronting was "bigger than a hamburger." She emphasized that the students were concerned not just with their own freedom, but with the "moral implications of racial discrimination for the 'whole world' and the 'Human Race.'" It was clear to her, and she hoped to make it clear through her article, that no one can be truly free while even one person still suffers under oppression. Baker also stressed the new group's focus on its own independence as an organization: "Desire for supportive cooperation from adult leaders and the adult community was also tempered by apprehension that adults might try to 'capture' the student movement. The students showed willingness to be met on the basis of equality, but were intolerant of anything that smacked of manipulation or domination."

Baker knew King hoped the students' organization might be a wing of the SCLC. But while King had given the opening keynote, it was Ella Baker who'd made a free space for the students' discussions and facilitated their dialogue. So her article made a clear statement: We learn from you, and we welcome your support, but do not try to tell us what to do.

The organization formed by the students that Easter weekend in Raleigh was dubbed the Student Nonviolent Coordinating Committee, or SNCC. It would become one of the most important and influential organizations in the struggle for Black freedom. SNCC played a key role in organizing the Freedom Rides, the March on Washington in 1963, and voter education and registration projects, including the Mississippi Freedom Summer. Baker had been right: the students already possessed the will and the courage to make change happen on their own.

In paying tribute to Baker after her death, her friend Anne Braden noted how pivotal Baker's confidence was to the student activists and grassroots workers with whom she shared meals and conversations late into the night. Baker had "tremendous faith in every human being whose life she touched . . . she gave people faith in themselves . . . and that's quite radical, because you can't build these movements without those people, individuals who believe in themselves." She had given the students reason to have confidence in their ability to effect change, to draw on the wisdom of their elders while letting them know that they were the ones best suited to know what needed to be done in their immediate, local situations.

At the time of the Southern Leadership Conference gathering, Baker was fifty-six years old—more than double the age of most of the participants. It had been decades since she was a student (as it happened, also at Shaw). But as she guided the students' conversations at the conference and throughout that summer, Baker was a welcome participant. Decades after the summer of 1960, those who were students and activists at the time would remember her unrelenting efforts to avoid getting propped up onto any pedestal. Ransby sets the scene:

> The small group of activists deliberated about the possibilities for the resurgent Black Freedom Movement while eating ice cream sundaes in the back room of B.B. Beamon's, Atlanta's legendary black-owned restaurant. Baker's personal regard for them endeared many of the young people in SNCC to her. She was clearly not a peer, but she was willing

to engage them on their turf, not just intellectually but socially too—over ice cream sundaes, in smoke-filled back rooms, or on long, uncomfortable rides in jalopies of various sorts. . . . Despite her age and encroaching health problems, Baker often rejected anything that could even remotely be construed as special treatment that would place distance between herself and the students. If they sat in uncomfortable chairs for long hours debating this or that, so would she. If they walked long distances, she walked with them at least as far as she could. If they slept in cramped accommodations on road trips, she did the same.

Others talked about sitting in rooms with her, everyone smoking, as she patiently listened to every person have a turn to voice their opinion. As she grew older, she found that the smoke irritated her lungs. But instead of requesting that they not smoke, or having them report back to her later, she simply got by as best she could, covering her mouth and nose, sometimes coughing surreptitiously, and listening with all of her might.

When I read about Baker, I think a lot about hospitality, about the role any act of hospitality implies for its two well-established relationships: host and guest. The host lays the table and invites those who will gather around it. The guests are the ones who come to partake of the host's generosity. At a dinner party, the role of the host is to keep the guests at ease, meet their needs, and help them feel welcome and wanted. The guests' role is to partake with gratefulness and enjoy the gathered company.

Usually the line between guest and host is clearly delineated. If you come to a party at my house, I'm the host. If I attend your wedding, I'm the guest.

But what made Baker so effective in her work was her ability to make that boundary between host and guest porous. Surely some of this ability stemmed from spending so much time as an "honored" guest in other people's kitchens, navigating the tension of being a welcome interloper taking part in a meal in an ordinary person's home while also holding a position of power that everyone recognized. It wasn't that Baker wanted to shrink into the background; it's that, by necessity, she had developed the ability to be a type of guest and host at the same time. She would eat someone else's food, listen to someone else's stories, sit at someone else's table, all with the need to make sure that they knew her position with the NAACP or SCLC or SNCC or any other organization didn't make her "better" than them, or more important than them. She, in effect, subtly learned the art of inhabiting the place of the host without usurping the role of the host.

And that carried over into the conferences and larger events Baker convened. She was never the main attraction, or at least she didn't think of herself that way; the people she brought together weren't really there to listen to her as much as to be listened to. And that is, in a sense, what the best facilitators or organizers do. They are creators of space, of sites for fellowship. And they carve out not just a physical place and time, but a phenomenological one. Baker believed a good space needs safety, boundaries set around it that create freedom within it—often a freedom that doesn't exist beyond the bounds of the space.

Priya Parker, a professional facilitator and strategic adviser, writes in her book *The Art of Gathering* that this requires understanding the role of the host as one of "generous authority":

> A gathering run on generous authority is run with a strong, confident hand, but it is run selflessly, for the sake of others. Generous authority is imposing in a way that serves your guests. . . . It spares them from the domination of some guests by other guests. . . . It wards off pretenders who threaten a purpose.

> Sometimes generous authority demands a willingness
> to be disliked in order to make your guests have the
> best experience of your gathering.

Baker certainly was a woman of generous authority, a person others listened to and learned from. Many of the people she affected—particularly but not only in SNCC—spoke of her as a teacher, partly through her words but primarily by example. She believed strongly in starting where people are, developing local leaders, leading from consensus, and making free spaces in which people could identify what their communities needed and then be empowered to do something about it.

But she was also the eternal guest-host, or perhaps host-guest, someone who knew the power of a shared meal and the best way to create space to invite people in. In that relationship is power. Experiencing freedom and security at someone's kitchen table— even your own—makes you imagine what the world could be like, and then, maybe, how to get there. Because, as Baker taught us, it's about a lot more than a hamburger and a giant, frosty Coke.

# FEAST
## LOUISIANA-STYLE SHRIMP SALAD

In 1959, after several years as interim director of the SCLC, Baker was exhausted. She wasn't the sort of woman to take breaks (although she loved a glass of whiskey or a bit of red wine to end the day). But she needed a vacation.

So after several weeks of organizing in Shreveport, she went to visit her friend Odette Harper Hines, who lived in Alexandria, Louisiana, not far away. The two had been friends for decades, having both lived in Harlem in the 1930s and having worked together with the NAACP in the 1940s.

But as Hines recounts in the biography she co-wrote with Judith Rollins, when Baker showed up, "her tongue was hanging out." Knowing her old friend well, Hines knew the remedy for burnout. She gave Baker some space to be alone and quiet for a while. And she also made Baker's favorite shrimp salad.

I can't say what exactly was in that shrimp salad. Shrimp salad recipes are a bit like chili recipes; every coastal region has its own spin on the dish. But it seems likely that Hines made a Louisiana-style salad, and Baker loved it. The basic recipe involves shrimp, mayonnaise, celery, bell pepper, and hard-boiled eggs, plus liquid crab boil (which, for the uninitiated, is a concentrated spicy liquid that's used in a traditional seafood boil). This is one way to make it. Everybody has their own, and everyone's got a story about their particular recipe.

### FOR THE SHRIMP

2 c. water

½ t. liquid crab boil (you can buy it on the internet if it's not in your grocery store, and a little goes a long way)

¼ t. salt

1 lb. shrimp, peeled

---

## For the Salad

3 hard-boiled eggs

1 stalk of celery

1 red bell pepper

1 green onion (aka scallion)

2 cloves of garlic

3 T. mayonnaise, with more on hand

3 T. lemon juice

½ t. salt

½ t. black pepper

1 T. minced parsley

Lettuce leaves and/or tomato slices

---

1. Put a big pot of water containing ¼ teaspoon salt and the liquid crab boil on the stove and bring to a boil. When it's rollicking, add the shrimp and cook for about 3–5 minutes; it's done when the shrimp turns pink. Drain the shrimp, then chill them in the refrigerator for half an hour.

2. Meanwhile, peel your hard-boiled eggs. Cut them in half and remove the yolks. Chop the whites into pieces.

3. Chop the celery, pepper, green onion, and garlic. Mince the parsley.

4. In a medium bowl, mix together the eggs, celery, pepper, green onion, garlic, lemon juice, ½ teaspoon salt, and black pepper.

5. Remove the shrimp from the fridge and chop them as well. Add them to the bowl and mix.

6. Add the mayonnaise and mix everything together again. Then add more mayonnaise till the consistency is to your liking. Add the parsley.

7. Now taste it and see if you need to add more of anything—salt, black pepper, garlic, even crushed red pepper if it's not spicy enough.

8. Once you're satisfied, put it in the refrigerator to chill.

9. When you're ready to serve, mold the salad over a bed of lettuce or tomato slices or both. Enjoy with chilled white wine, or maybe some sweet tea (if you add a shot of Jim Beam, I won't tell). Rest your feet, take a breather, and listen to someone's story.

# More Salt with Ella Baker

*Ella Baker and the Black Freedom Movement*, by Barbara Ransby: A stunner of a book that functions not just as a deeply researched chronicle of Baker's life but also as a primer on the varying veins of activism present in the Civil Rights Movement of the twentieth century.

*Ella Baker's Catalytic Leadership: A Primer on Community Engagement and Communication for Social Justice*, by Patricia S. Parker: A leading activist-scholar explores how Baker's legacy inspires and informs her own activism today, using several case studies to illuminate her praxis.

*Ella Baker: Community Organizer of the Civil Rights Movement*, by Todd Moye: A basic introduction to Baker's life, which traces how she became an organizer and her impact on the world.

SNCC Digital Gateway: Ella Baker (snccdigital.org/people/ella-baker): A website created by SNCC, the organization Baker helped found, that tells Baker's story and includes video tributes to Baker from people who knew her.

ELiZaBeTH DAVID

## CHAPTER FIVE

# ELIZABETH DAVID

## DIRTY WORDS AND FUTURE JOY

The winter of 1946–47 in England was so brutally and unusually cold, the weather so nasty, that getting heating fuel to London was difficult, and shipments often came late. One chilly London resident was Elizabeth David, recently returned to her native country after seven years living abroad in sunnier climates.

Even without the terrible cold, English living would have been dismal that winter; the war had ended over a year earlier, but austerity measures were still in place, and the foods that could help make a miserable season more bearable—eggs, butter, milk, sugar, meat— were still subject to rationing. For years already, cooks and housewives had scraped together dinner from what was available, using "austerity cookbooks" that advised making faux marzipan from beans and almond extract, and "brains," a dinner staple, from leftover porridge, an onion, and an egg.

David had ridden out the war in warm places, like the Mediterranean, Egypt, and even briefly in India. She'd often lacked resources, but she found that the food she ate in those places was both affordable and vibrant. "What I found out when I returned to England to another five or six years of the awful dreary foods of rationing was that while my own standard of living in Egypt had perhaps not been very high, my food had always had some sort of life, color, guts, stimulus; there had always been bite, flavor, and inviting smells," she wrote in 1960. "These elements were totally absent from English meals."

Shivering in her wardrobe of warm-weather clothes, David finally decamped for a hotel in Ross-on-Wye, near Hereford, over a hundred miles from London, because she hoped it would have at least some heat, and as she wrote years later, "That was miracle enough." (She also brought a man with her, but she didn't mention him in her future writing, probably because she was married to someone else at the time.)

There in Ross-on-Wye, she started walking around during the day, exploring the town, which was full of pubs, sometimes called public houses. Many of them served local Hereford cider, "most of it rough, some very rough indeed." Food in such establishments was scarce, but at least it was something to do. It was on one of these walks that she stumbled across a shop selling some kitchen implements. And for a lark, David bought a dish and a white jug with the silhouette of the head of John Wesley, the evangelist and founder of Methodism, printed on the side.

She considered moving on from Ross-on-Wye, but nasty weather made traveling treacherous, and so she stayed, stuck in this small town. By then, the food had become, as she remembered it later, "very difficult indeed to swallow." Her descriptions make it clear why: "There was flour and water soup seasoned solely with pepper; bread and gristle rissoles"—a rissole is a patty, in this case made from the nasty ends of cuts of meat, encased in pastry and baked or deep-fried—"dehydrated onions and carrots;

corned beef toad-in-the-hole. I need not go on. We all know that kind of cooking. It still exists."

To make matters worse, when you stayed at a hotel more than a night or two, you handed over your rations book to the management, who would use the coupons to buy the food they'd in turn "cook" for you. So it wasn't possible to just leave the hotel and go buy something edible at the supermarket. It was cold, it was wet, and she was stuck and hungry and miserable.

Well, there was one thing to do. Until then, David—who would go on to reshape English appetites and become one of the most famous and influential food writers of her time—hadn't written much of anything, let alone recipes. She'd studied art, dabbled in acting, run a library in Cairo, and traveled farther than many of her peers, and along the way she'd developed a taste for fresh, seasonal food and learned to cook it even with limited resources. There in the hotel, she gathered her memories of those experiences.

Perhaps that's all she needed.

"Hardly knowing what I was doing," she later wrote, "I who had scarcely ever put pen to paper except to write memos to the heads of departments in the Ministry which employed me during the war, I sat down and, watched over by John Wesley, started to work out an agonized craving for the sun and a furious revolt against that terrible, cheerless, heartless food by writing down descriptions of Mediterranean and Middle Eastern cuisine."

It's impossible to know precisely what she composed in those first days. But the recollections she set to paper to rebel against the misery of flour-and-water soup were the seeds from which David's first book sprung, titled *A Book of Mediterranean Food* and published in 1950. It's a recipe book heavy with an air of remembering, of calling up sensual experiences and translating them into something the reader, too, can experience. Opening the book at random reveals passages like this one—part instruction, part sighing memoir:

### STUFFED TOMATOES À LA GRECQUE

Displayed in enormous round shallow pans, these tomatoes, together with pimentos and small marrows cooked in the same way, are a feature of every Athenian taverna, where one goes into the kitchen and chooses one's meal from the pans arrayed on the stove. It is impossible to describe the effect of the marvellous smells which assail one's nose, and the sight of all those bright-coloured concoctions is overwhelming. Peering into every stewpan, trying a spoonful of this, a morsel of that, it is easy to lose one's head and order a dish of everything on the menu.

Cut off the tops of a dozen large tomatoes, scoop out the flesh and mix it with 2 cups of cooked rice. To this mixture add 2 tablespoons of chopped onion, 2 tablespoons of currants, some chopped garlic, pepper, salt, and, if you have it, some left-over lamb or beef. Stuff the tomatoes with this mixture and bake them in a covered dish in the oven, with olive oil.

No matter that in those days, you could hardly get fresh tomatoes or meat, and that English cooks were highly suspicious of garlic, which wouldn't have been widely available either. The same suspicion held for olive oil; it would be decades before it became a staple from London to Leeds. So her recipe-like passages read as pure fantasy. David didn't mind. Her aim, she wrote in the introduction to the book, was "to give some idea of the lovely cookery of those regions to people who do not already know them, and to stir the memories of those who have eaten this food on its native shores, and who would like sometimes to bring a flavour of those blessed lands of sun and sea and olive trees into their English kitchens." She offered delicious, delicious fantasy.

In 1963, recounting that cold winter and her act of implausible revolt for the readers of *The Spectator*, David wrote that "even to write words like apricot, olives and butter, rice and lemons, oil and almonds, produced assuagement. Later I came to realize that in the England of 1947, those were dirty words that I was putting down."

According to David's biographer, Artemis Cooper, all that lousy hotel food "unleashed the source of the creative rage" that drove David's writing:

> In that miserably cold winter of 1947, she found the heart of her own blazing fire. Of course, she did not always write in the white heat of passion: there is no point wasting emotional energy on custard powder and gravy mix. But whenever she tweaked the noses of pompous restaurateurs, laughed at a factory-made pie or poked fun at the sacred cows of British cookery, she was tapping into the same incandescent exasperation that drove her to put pen to paper in Ross-on-Wye.

*Apricot, butter, oil*, and *lemon* would continue to be dirty words for a while longer. Even when *A Book of Mediterranean Food* was released, five years after the end of the war, rationing was still in place. It wouldn't be fully over till 1954, when the meat ration came to a close. By then David had published her second book, *French Country Cooking*, with *Italian Food* on its way. Each of them challenged English cooks—not known for their adventuresome cuisine, worn down by cooking in dire circumstances—to now expand their palates and seek out new ingredients. Her books burst with colors, textures, spices, smells, flavors, and possibilities. She filled them with recipes, keen and vivid descriptions, and literary passages from other writers.

Reading one of David's books was itself a meal, and something more as well: an opportunity to indulge the imagination, to think of a future world in which rationing had ended, the horrors and anxieties of war in the past. New experiences were everywhere, beckoning a weary country to experience delight again.

|||||||||||||||||||||||||||||||

The early months of the COVID-19 pandemic coincided with my early work on the book in your hands. In my hometown of New York, many of us felt that first spring like we'd never left the winter—the sadness, the loss, the limited groceries, the barren store shelves. The late-dawning sun outside did little to dispel the clouds inside many of our souls, the fruits of a devastating season with hundreds of thousands of lives already lost around the world and more to pass, and ugly realities unveiled that some of us were accustomed to ignoring.

In photos of New York City from that miserable time, you can see a city where infections spiked so rapidly that field hospitals appeared in Central Park and refrigerated trucks—additional morgue space—were parked outside of hospitals, which felt exactly like something from a movie. To be a resident of New York in April 2020 was to spend all day and night listening to sirens, to discover—as my husband and I did—that the reason nobody had collected the garbage in the hallway for weeks was that the kindly superintendent had contracted the disease and died, and in the ensuing chaos residents hadn't been informed. The two of us were among the lucky; we were able to stay home, and we didn't get sick. But all around us was loss. If you didn't lose a family member, you knew people who did, and those who kept the city going were suddenly disappearing. It was awful, frightening, and exhausting.

Home cooks and food writers leaned heavily on pantry food. Aisles of essential items and staples were sold out before we made it to the store that first spring. Scarcity, not abundance, was what we felt. And as we kept squinting down the tunnel, looking for hope, no one could know what would come next.

We made it through that first year somehow. But it was during those months that I became engrossed with Elizabeth David's life and work, and I felt a kinship, like we were in a similar boat as she was when she started writing. It felt like we were stuck in gray, cold, rainy Ross-on-Wye in the winter of 1947, and we desperately needed to close our eyes and recall what goodness felt like.

||||||||||||||||||||||||||||||||||

Elizabeth David was not always a cook, and certainly not a food writer. Long before she was penning odes to stuffed tomatoes and garlic, she was born the daughter of a conservative member of Parliament who later was appointed government minister, and she grew up amidst relative wealth. Young Elizabeth wouldn't have learned to cook; that was a job for the household staff. She was interested in art.

In 1930, her mother—now a widow—sent teenage Elizabeth to Paris to study art at the Sorbonne (where Agnès Varda would later study literature and psychology). David didn't like her studies very much, but years later, in *French Country Cooking*, she recalled what she had learned from the family she boarded with. It wasn't art. "What had stuck was the taste for a kind of food quite ideally unlike anything I had known before," she wrote. With a jocular tone, she recounted their love of food, and of the table. That love stuck with her. (She wouldn't be the last Anglophone to be jolted into life by the French culinary experience.)

As a young woman born to a wealthy family with connections to the aristocracy, David was expected to go through the traditional social rituals for people of her station. She was presented at court as a debutante and attended grand balls. But either David didn't fancy any of the young men she met, or—as her biographers suggest—her wit and sharp tongue put them off. It didn't matter; David had decided to become an actress.

From there, her life took a winding path, marked by good times, passionate affairs, and a search for adventure and purpose. It turned out she wasn't particularly good at acting either, but as part of her move to London to join the Open Air Theatre at Regent's Park, she took a set of rooms in a shared house near the park and learned to cook for herself. It was the early 1930s, fifteen years before that cold and fateful winter.

Eventually she started seeing a fellow actor, Charles Gibson Cowan, swarthy, married, working-class, and nine years her senior. David's mother tried to break up their relationship, sending David to Malta and later to Egypt in 1936, but that only lasted a short while. Soon David returned to England to work briefly in fashion (which she also hated), before leaving for southern France and Corsica. After some time, she came back to England and reunited with Cowan. In 1939, they bought a boat together and set sail for Greece. She wouldn't come back for seven years.

But Greece proved hard to get to. They'd crossed the English Channel and sailed through a network of canals in France, reaching Marseilles. But then war broke out, and they could only get from Marseilles to Antibes before they were halted, unable to obtain permission from the government to leave. In Antibes, they lived on the boat for six months, stuck in a bureaucratic holding pattern, with nothing to do but wait.

As often happens on the road, Cowan and David were growing tired of one another, but fortunately, David met someone
who would become very important to her: the writer Norman
Douglas, who was many decades her senior. The pair became
inseparable, dining together constantly, Douglas showing her
all of his most cherished Antibes haunts and delicacies. Later,
she would say that he taught her to seek out the best in everything, to insist on the freshest ingredients and finest foods she
could afford. And while people would someday speculate that
she had been in love with him, others suggested it was the affection of a student for a mentor rather than a romance, though it
was undoubtedly suffused with romantic flourishes of wonder
for twenty-something Elizabeth.

When the time came for David and Cowan to sail on, having
finally gained permission to cast off, Douglas gave her a copy of
his book *Old Calabria*. In the front, he wrote, "Always do as you
please, and send everybody to Hell, and take the consequences."
She had found a kindred spirit.

The next few years took David through several countries and
particularly rough times, as the war seethed all around them.
Her relationship with Cowan broke up amicably. She found
work for the British government, first in Alexandria, then in
Cairo, where she ran a reference library for the British Ministry
of Information. And from the cooks she hired, she learned how
to make food that was wholly different from the English food of
her youth.

According to David, it was the custom of her fellow English
countrymen (and women) to view Spanish food as boring, Italian
food as heavy and lacking in imagination, and French food as
worthy of an eyebrow raise. As Clarissa Dickson Wright explains
in her foreword to the 2002 edition of *A Book of Mediterranean
Food*, "You must remember that at the time this book was written

the British regarded foreign food as 'filth.'" An English meal was merely a piece of meat served with two vegetables and potatoes, no more, no less.

While learning how to eat from Douglas and later how to make food from the local cooks she hired in Egypt, David—who clearly was not fond of English customs to begin with—permitted her palate to grow by leaps and bounds. She found that doing so also challenged her notions of "foreign"-ness. Could British prejudice against certain foods be keeping them from delicious possibility? Were *they* the narrow-minded ones? In a chapter on various types of meats in Mediterranean cuisine, when writing about baby goats, she is at pains to challenge her readers:

> The meat of young kid is much appreciated all over the Mediterranean, especially in the more primitive parts such as Corsica and the Greek islands. It is hard to say why there is such a prejudice against this animal in England, and it is only the gastronomically ignorant who, the moment they go abroad, suppose that whatever meat they are eating is disguised horse or goat. . . .
>
> In the same way, foreigners in the Middle East are often heard to complain that they are being served with camel instead of beef. If they had ever eaten camel meat they would soon know the difference.

And then, with a wink to her readers, she's on to the next chapter, titled *Boar*.

David has no desire to convince the midcentury English housewife to rush out and buy a tender baby goat. She almost certainly could not, even if she wanted to. Instead, she offers her readers the image of a bigger life, in which the reader might tour Corsica on holiday and properly enjoy a shoulder of kid stuffed with a mix of other meats, some spinach, an egg, all served over polenta while the sun sets over the sea. To savor life, to smack one's lips at the dream of a rich, bountiful world.

|||||||||||||||||||||||||||||||||

After she left Egypt, David's life got messy. She had many affairs while she was in Cairo, until she met an army officer, Tony David, whom she didn't particularly love but who represented stability. So she married him and followed him to India. There she did not much like the food or, to be perfectly honest, her husband, whom she found to be feckless and a spendthrift.

Eventually she had a severe attack of sinusitis, and in the summer of 1946, on the order of doctors who feared she'd get worse in the Indian summer heat, she went home to England. Her husband followed her there, but the marriage was more or less over. And while she had other relationships over the years (including the great love of her life, Peter Higgins, who broke her heart when he married someone else), her return to England marked a turning point for David: from then on, she was, for the most part, her own person.

And she became famous, at least in her native England, as well as to the American cooks and writers (like M.F.K. Fisher, Julia Child, and Alice Waters) who found inspiration in her love of *terroir*, the French term for the taste of a region as it manifests in its food. Her food books sold well, but she also wrote columns in newspapers and magazines, bringing her signature style and snap to all sorts of topics. She extolled to her readers the virtues of specific open-air markets in France (Agnès Varda would have been pleased) and preparations of virtually every kind of food one can imagine. And as England emerged into the 1960s, locals began to clamor for ingredients from Egypt, Italy, France, and elsewhere. Thanks to David's writing, people wanted to taste the food she described not only in their minds but on their tongues as well. She'd won them over, and now they wanted good olive oil, brought in from the Mediterranean.

David's columns kept generations enthralled, with their often hilarious and quite personal writing. She'd take trips to France and Italy for research, driving around with friends, filing articles bemoaning the state of a small restaurant she once loved or sharing a new find with her readers. Manufacturers of packaged foods in postwar England, understanding David's growing influence, would send her foods to try. She did not look on those samples with much kindness. In one column titled "Lucky Dip," published in *The Spectator* in June 1962, she surgically eviscerated a ready-made pie that had arrived on her doorstep for her to try and, the company had hoped, promote:

> True, I did once offer the filling of one of these pies (chicken, veal, flour, edible fats, seasoning, milk powder, flavouring, phosphate. Preheat oven to a hot condition. Remove lid of can) to my cat, and whether it was the chicken or the veal or the flavouring or the phosphate, or was it just that I hadn't got the oven to a sufficiently hot condition, she took to it no more than she did to that pair of frankfurters which arrived in the post one early morning after they'd spent a long weekend at the offices of the magazine for which I was then writing, and were thoughtfully packed with a tube of mustard. Come to think of it, it was the mustard they were pushing, not the sausages. That very same post brought, if I remember rightly, a jar of crab paste and a chromium-plated fork for creaming synthetic lard.

That sounds disgusting, but her prose is delicious, as are her reviews of books she felt were ridiculous or unnecessary, and her jaunty accounts of meals gone awry at fancy English places. All columnists have those few topics they return to again and again, and David's were the need for the English to expand their palates, and the decisive need to seek out fresh, simple ingredients, season them properly, and serve them with an eye to presentation (something she learned from her travels). But the plethora of ways she presented these ideas, and the winsome, sometimes even stern voice in which they're written, make her feel like someone you want to please.

Despite the liveliness of David's prose and the adventures abroad she recounted in columns, her life was not easy. She was disappointed in love. Her family members suffered through terrible health problems, both mental and physical. David herself suffered from depression, illness (including tuberculosis), a horrible car accident, and eventually a stroke. In 1963, while she was at the height of her powers as a food writer, she had a cerebral hemorrhage, which left her with a severely reduced sense of taste—an almost incomprehensible loss for someone whose entire livelihood was predicated on the joys of taste.

What she did next was brave. She could have given up writing about cooking, but instead she pivoted to exploring food history. Her interest in the many regional Italian cuisines came from knowing that they each grew out of a vast history dating back to ancient Rome. So in new books on bread, and on ice and frozen confections, she revealed traditions readers could become part of by making those same things at home instead of buying factory-bought bread or store-bought ice cream. She wanted you to share in the richness of the world. For David, the world was an interconnected place full of cultures that had flowed into one another over time and space. She rejoiced in what she learned from others, whether or not they shared a language or a heritage or traditions of food. She would not have been an isolationist.

That is probably among the reasons she devoted so much column and book space to the cooks and restaurateurs (especially women) who shared their recipes with her, both at home and abroad. One essay collected in her book *An Omelette and a Glass of Wine* is titled "Mafalda, Giovanna, Giulia," because those are the names of the women who gave their recipes to her for the essay. Mafalda, who ran a restaurant with her husband in southern Italy, showed David how to buy and preserve pimentos. Giovanna, a young girl, cooked spaghetti with chicken livers and lemon in Chianti, Tuscany; David declares her to be "a most original and gifted pasta cook." And Giulia, a Tuscan woman, gave David a recipe for Riso Ricco, a hot rice dish rich with a butter-and-egg sauce. "Giulia's cooking was like herself, elegant and delicate," she writes. Going to school for formal training in the culinary arts was not important. What mattered was what you could cook. (Or not cook; "In France, no shame is attached to buying ready-prepared food because most of it is of high quality," David writes, extolling the institution of the French charcutier.)

David's friends remembered her as being occasionally prickly but always generous. In 1965, she opened a shop that bore her name, Elizabeth David Ltd., which sold carefully selected kitchen implements, many of which were imported and which she helped make popular in England. She eventually fell out with her partners—she had prioritized the quality of what she stocked over actually making money—but the shop continued on, bearing her name and making its mark, and David did, too. A former employee, Rosi Hanson, told a journalist that "she was good fun, and the shop was magical. She rather loved being a shopkeeper, perhaps because it gave her a rest from writing. If someone wanted some very specific piece of equipment, I often heard her say: 'If you could come back, I think I may have one at home.'"

And if you came for an afternoon meal at her home, you'd find yourself in a kitchen with a long table. At one end, she wrote on her typewriter. At the other, you'd be served lunch. Nothing fancy; probably an omelette and a glass of wine. But she trusted you to taste the possibility, to understand the perfect prospect of hope in a few eggs, some good butter, and a couple of vegetables folded into a silky bundle. David was not lavish or excessive, at least not when it came to what she ate on a daily basis. Her nephew Jonathan Gray once said that his aunt "was quite an ascetic person, not at all greedy," and wondered why she never left England permanently, given she was always side-eyeing British food. (Her essays are littered with annoyance at what had happened to the glorious, simple Italian pizza in English hands.)

But David's daily preference for simplicity and a life in a country just climbing out of austerity makes sense, to me. A luxurious banquet with the finest wines and the most beautiful food money can buy has its place. But that place is rarely, if ever, at the kitchen table. That doesn't mean the alternative must be nasty packaged pie and roast beef cooked till it's gray, powdered eggs and bread that tastes like nothing. David entreated her readers to learn from their neighbors—to find hope in a tomato, joy in fine olive oil, love in a clove of garlic.

We emerge, over and over, from nasty seasons of one kind or another. I am emerging from one now, and thinking of you, who are likely doing the same as I write this, wherever you are. It won't be the last long winter we live through, nor the last time when everything tastes like flour and water with a little black pepper. When we've become accustomed to the tasteless and the tough for so long, it's hard to imagine the future as briny, aromatic, succulent, and salty, bursting with flavor and joy.

But here we are, and we can do what Elizabeth David did: create a bulwark against the dark. It is no longer difficult to buy garlic or olive oil in English supermarkets; Mediterranean and Middle Eastern food, cooked by those who see David as their kitchen-godmother, is easy to find everywhere in London. Her remembering was generative, giving birth to something new that was also old at the very same time. After all, David's "dirty words" of hope did more than comfort her—they changed the eating and cooking habits of a whole country and, in some sense, the world.

So, too, we remember. We can recount to one another our memories of abundance. Say them like a litany, a prayer: apricot, olives, and butter, rice and lemons, almonds and oil. Then add your own: salty Dutch licorice, a peppery red wine, empanadas and plantain chips, a bowl of green curry, a steaming pot of ramen. David's writing is just a sliver of the legacy she left us, but she gave us the words to carry on her work.

# FEAST
## MOULES MARINIÈRE, THREE WAYS

This recipe appears, more or less, in *A Book of Mediterranean Food* as Moules Marinière. "There are several versions of *moules marinière*," David writes, and then offers three of them.

I chose this recipe to represent David for a couple reasons. One is that it incorporates some of her favorite ingredients, including garlic and a glass of white wine. I can imagine her eating this dish with gusto, perhaps near the Mediterranean, where the mussels are fresh, large, juicy, and delicious.

The other reason, though, is that mussels give me the same sensation I get reading David's work—that of being completely satisfied. It took me a while after moving to New York in my early twenties to realize I was now living on an island and fresh seafood was plentiful and easy to get. But it wasn't until 2015, when I spent my first six weeks in Paris, that I really understood mussels.

One day, starving for some lunch and finding most restaurants closed (it was Sunday), my husband and I stumbled on a Belgian restaurant called Académie de la Bière, on the Boulevard de Port-Royal in Montparnasse. It's a brasserie with copious *al fresco* dining (if I can swap my languages for a moment); they serve a few different cuisines, but their specialty—besides a lot of different and lovely beers (not easy to find in Paris), many made by monks—is big, heaping, savory, steaming bowls of mussels, prepared six different ways. There's a blue cheese preparation, *au Roquefort*, and a stunning curry mussels bowl, but my favorite is still the simplest—*moules marinière*, in garlic and butter and white wine.

Right now I can close my eyes and almost, *almost* inhale the fragrance. The day we first went to the restaurant, it happened to be a bit cold and rainy, and we were so hungry. The bowls of mussels and tall, Belgian beers were the greatest meal I'd ever tasted in my life. So whenever we're in Paris, one of our first stops is always Académie de la Bière, for mussels and crusty French bread and a half-liter of hearty beer.

Lately, I've been quite literally dreaming about being in Paris again. About mussels and beer. But while I wait, like Elizabeth David in Ross-on-Wye, I am trying to conjure the feeling by writing about food, and making it too.

David's recipes are not easy to follow all the time, so I've rewritten her three preparations to make them a little more step-by-step for the mussels newbie. But don't worry: there's almost nothing easier to make than mussels. Just make sure you get them fresh and cold—preferably from someone at a farmers' market if you can; it's always good to befriend a local fishmonger—and try to cook them the same day.

---

3 quarts mussels (about 4 lb.), cleaned. To clean mussels, dump them into a colander in your sink. Grab a brush and scrub the outside of the shells with medium force to clear away ocean debris; you may still end up with some things clinging to the shells, but do the best you can. Tap any open mussels lightly, and if they don't close within a few seconds, throw them out; that one's dead already and might make you sick. Trust me.

1 small onion, chopped finely

1 clove of garlic, chopped (you can use more! I always triple the garlic!)

¾ c. white wine (a dry one is best; you can serve the rest
with the meal)

1 stalk of celery, chopped

1 bunch of parsley, chopped

2 T. butter

4 T. flour

Bread to dip in the broth (baguette is great, or a hearty
country loaf)

---

## Preparation I

1. In a large, deep pot (I use a stock pot), combine
the onion, garlic, and celery. Add white wine and 2
cups of water. Sprinkle in some black pepper.

2. Add the mussels, turn the burner to high, and cover
the pot. After 2 minutes, stir the mussels. Give
them another 6–8 minutes and their shells should
have opened.

3. When the mussels open, using a slotted spoon or
tongs, take them out of the pot and put them somewhere they can stay warm (another pot with a cover
is good, or a tureen with a cover). Add butter and
flour to the liquid in the pot, stir, and cook till it
thickens a little and looks like a tasty sauce; this
will not take very long.

4. Dish up the mussels into individual bowls or
place in a serving dish. Pour the sauce over them.
Sprinkle with parsley and eat immediately, with
the best bread you can find to dip in the sauce.

## PREPARATION 2

1. David says that another way to do this is to make the sauce first. Put the butter, flour, onion, celery, garlic, and white wine into the pot; add 2 cups water; and cook over high heat.

2. When the liquid "has the consistency of a thin soup," add the mussels.

3. After the mussels open, they should be served immediately, which she says is "a great advantage, as they then do not lose their freshness and savor, which they are apt to do if they are reheated."

4. However, she warns—and this could be tricky— "on no account must the sauce be over-thickened, or you will simply have mussels in a white sauce." So, be careful. (And perhaps use preparation 1.)

## PREPARATION 3

1. Although David describes this as "the most unusual way," it's also the way I'm most familiar with from Académie de la Bière. Put the mussels into the pot with the wine, but no water.

2. Heat over high heat; as they heat, sprinkle the parsley, onion, and garlic over them.

3. When the mussels open, all the ingredients have been steamed, and you can just serve them. There won't be as much delicious broth, so you could elect to add some broth to the white wine after you've transferred the mussels to the bowls.

No matter which preparation you choose, serve them with white wine or mineral water, along with bread and butter. This should serve about four people. A good rule of thumb is 1 pound of mussels per person. It will look like a lot, but don't worry; it's a light supper, best eaten outside as the sun is just beginning to lower in the sky, and with the most care and attention you can give to the goodness of these ingredients and how they come together. It tastes like hope.

# MORE SALT WITH ELIZABETH DAVID

*A Book of Mediterranean Food*: David's books are all good, but her first is a special delight and probably the best place to start, since it was her first book. (New York Review Books has been bringing out editions of David's books, and they're lovely, inexpensive, and accessible reading.)

*An Omelette and a Glass of Wine*: This anthology collects many of David's magazine and newspaper columns. It showcases her signature wit, humor, and deadpan critique of cookery books and restaurants of the time. It's a lot of fun.

*Writing at the Kitchen Table: The Authorized Biography of Elizabeth David*, by Artemis Cooper, and *Elizabeth David: A Mediterranean Passion*, by Lisa Cheney: Two biographies of David, both comprehensive. David's life is so interesting that even when the biographies get into the weeds, they're still totally enjoyable.

## CHAPTER SIX

# OCTAVIA BUTLER

## THE HUMAN CONTRADICTION

Of all the women seated around the table at
this imaginary dinner party I've convened, Octavia Butler may seem like
the most surprising choice. She'd fit
right in at any gathering devoted
to sharing ideas and stories, but
she's not known for her lessons
on eating and drinking. A
science-fiction writer, and
considered by many to be
the mother of Afrofuturism,
Butler rarely placed food
center stage in her novels, nor
did she write cookbooks or travel-
ogues. She wasn't known for boisterous
cocktail parties or boozy salons, and she didn't organize direct action
around kitchen tables.

Though her novels reveal conflicted feelings about humanity,
Butler was generous with journalists and interested in the people
around her. However, she also valued her solitude, describing herself to interviewers as "comfortably asocial." In 1998, she explained to
journalist Mike McGonigal that she liked "spending most of my time
alone. I enjoy people best if I can be alone much of the time. I used to

worry about it because my family worried about it. And I finally realized: This is the way I am. That's that. We all have some weirdness, and this is mine."

In interviews from the 1980s and '90s, Butler revealed that her cheerful status as a loner who occasionally came out to socialize actually came from a deeper loneliness. When she was born in 1947, her parents had already lost four sons at or near birth. Her mother was a domestic worker, on her feet all day; she was widowed shortly after Butler was born and dreamed that little Estelle Octavia might someday grow up to have a secretarial job so she would have the chance to sit at work. Butler described herself as feeling like an outsider, an "out-kid," in her Pasadena community. "I think I was called ugly in first grade, and I went on being called ugly all the way through junior high school," she told a pair of interviewers in 1997. She'd been "an only child and never really learned to work with other people very well." So, like many loners before her, she found refuge in the world of words, stories, and ideas. And yet, for her, writing was more than merely an escape from a lonely world.

Butler often downplayed her clear skills as a writer, emphasizing that she had to work tirelessly at it. As a Black and female voice, she knew the racism and biases that marked the genre, which is often written for and dominated by white men. But she was also determined to support herself with her writing, to make her way in the world by selling and publishing her stories.

For much of her life, Butler scraped by financially. She made scores of intricate lists and budgets to ensure that she could survive on what she made at temp jobs. Even after she sold her first book (*Patternmaster*, published in 1976), she felt like she was always waiting on checks to arrive, always worried the money was about to run out. A typical budget scratched out on the back of an envelope might detail the groceries she needed, calculated to the cent: "pepper, onions, tomatoes, envelopes, taco sauce, nacho, can beans, tortillas, cheese," which came to $11.59. It was still a lot. She looked into getting food stamps.

But through that anxiety, through the daily clanging of rent and food insecurity—one of the most isolating experiences a person can have—she never stopped writing. She made lists and schedules of what she needed to do, and wrote out contracts with herself that renewed her commitment to her work. She got up at 2:00 a.m. so she could write before catching the bus to work, because despite living in the Los Angeles area and later in Seattle, Butler never learned to drive—she took the bus everywhere.

And she knew where to find a feast. Butler treasured the Pasadena Library more than any other place: it was her true home, her free space, her lifeline, a never-ending buffet of riches for a richly curious mind. Even when she became a well-known, sought-after author, no longer worried about affording a can of beans and taco sauce, she went to the library for what she called "grazing": wandering around a new section, some unfamiliar place in the stacks, looking for new books and new ideas. She did this, she told Charles Rowell in 1997, "to whet my appetite when I am shopping for new ideas."

Butler's hard-won wisdom about creating, and her insatiable curiosity, are a large part of why I envision her at this dinner party table. It's absolutely clear from her work that she's ravenous—which is to say, she simply cannot stop reading and learning. She speaks and writes fluidly and knowledgeably about matters ranging from biodeterminism to feminism, the history of slavery to present-day oppression of Mexican migrant workers, Reagan's nuclear policy to the possibility that humanity's future lies elsewhere in the solar system. She watched people on the bus, listened to their conversations, noted their behavior. She read books of names in preparation for future characters, making note of monikers that carried symbolic significance. She frequently called herself a "news junkie," advising one young interviewer (future *New Yorker* writer Jelani Cobb) to listen to NPR. She loved dictionaries.

As a result, her writing is radical and unapologetic, a bold, proud challenge to the white, male-dominated vision of the future that science fiction often produces. Her interest in everything—the whole of the universe—isn't the behavior of a dilettante. Nor does it stem from some need to sound smart at a dinner party, to wow her fellow guests. When Butler speaks, even from her deep well of knowledge, these topics arise naturally. They're always swimming around in her mind.

So, I suspect Butler's "happy asociality" is a strategy that lets her focus the grand library of knowledge she's absorbed on her work, her characters, and her exploration of what it means to be human. Reading her novels is like sitting in a diner with a fascinating and passionate woman, letting her lead you through a conversation that sprawls from lunch into dinner and then into the night. She tells you about the latest book she's plucked from the library shelves, the things she's been learning, and she asks you how we might make our way through this messy world alongside one another.

And she tells you about something she's been mulling, something she calls "the human contradiction." It sounds to you like a play on the phrase "human condition," so she explains further. Humans, she says, are brilliant creatures—that much is clear just from a tour around the riches in her beloved library. They can build almost anything they can imagine, create heartbreaking and mind-blowing works of art, raise families, dream up theories to explain the universe, engineer crops that could end world hunger, map the deepest oceans, even walk on the moon.

But even with all of that brilliance, they're driven, most often, not toward bettering the whole of humanity, but toward accruing power and drawing boundaries between their group and some "out-group." Despite the richness of their intellectual capabilities, humans seem incapable of defining the world in terms other than stark binaries: us and them, the good and the bad, the ones who deserve to live well and the ones who don't matter. And for many humans, the "in-group," the one I personally belong to, is the one that deserves power.

That's the human contradiction, she tells you, and if history tells us anything, this contradiction constantly threatens the ongoing life and health of the species. Our lust for power leads us to commit atrocities, build world-ending bombs, wreck the planet in pursuit of wealth, allow some people to starve while others throw away food, and much, much more. Every day's news headlines make that more clear. This, she says, is what drives her to write science fiction: the ability to see that human contradiction and place it in terms of the past, the present, and the uncertain future and, perhaps, to imagine a better way.

When the waitstaff finally starts pushing the broom around, you stumble out through the doors, fully sated and yet wishing for more. She heads to the bus stop and you start walking home, turning over what she said in your mind. And though you may not realize it at the moment, not only has she given you a lot to think about—she's been observing you, too.

IIIIIIIIIIIIIIIIIIIIIIIIIIIIIIIII

Most of Butler's characters are just trying to survive, which makes the role food plays in her novels interesting. It's rarely sumptuous or a sensual delight. And when it does show up, it's almost always there to show us the threat and potential promise of the human contradiction.

Many of Butler's novels center a protagonist—often a Black woman—who finds herself alone in the world, or at least alone in *a* world. Beset by challenges she barely understands, she has to improvise and stay focused to survive, and to lead others to survival. Those around her, meanwhile, threaten not just her single-mindedness, but her very life.

Take Lilith Ayepo, for instance, for whom Butler's trilogy *Lilith's Brood*—consisting of *Dawn* (1987), *Adulthood Rites* (1988), and *Imago* (1989)—is named. Lilith's story starts several centuries after humans have nearly wiped themselves out in a catastrophic nuclear war. An alien race called the Oankali rescue the humans from the earth's surface and, to buy time, put the humans into a deep sleep on their "ship," a biologically complex organism that's more like a planet than a spacecraft. Then the Oankali set about repairing the earth's surface, restoring it from a radioactive wasteland to a primordial state. They also start "investigating" the humans, looking into their cellular structure to understand their biology. They are fascinated by human genomes, illnesses, and neural pathways; they find aberrations like cancers, which they can heal on the spot, to be captivating sources of information they can file away for future use.

Lilith, a Black woman from California, is among those who were taken to their ship. She's all alone; her husband and son died during the nuclear war. The Oankali put her to sleep for around 250 years, awakening her from time to time and then putting her back under while they investigate her biology. As *Dawn*, the first book in the trilogy, opens, they've decided to awaken Lilith and gently but inescapably conscript her into helping them prepare the first small group of humans to return to the recently restored earth and begin a fresh chapter in the planet's story.

The Oankali think of themselves as traders. If they come to a planet, or a species, they wish to both take things (like genes) and give things in return. In the case of humans, they bring healing and a project: creating an "upgraded" human race. Thanks to the human contradiction, humans almost wiped themselves out, but the Oankali—who see in humanity something worth preserving—are certain they can find a way to fix those deficiencies.

But while the Oankali consider themselves traders, their "trades" with the humans aren't really voluntary—they're coercive. Humans are put to sleep and investigated without consent. And the Oankali have no desire to simply set them loose on the earth before they've altered them—humans will just repeat the same errors. The Oankali have a plan for humanity, and, no matter their good intentions, the humans don't have much choice in the matter. (Ella Baker, who believed in letting communities direct their own empowerment, would definitely, *definitely* not approve.)

In the *Lilith's Brood* novels, meals are where the power imbalance between Oankali and humans comes into sharp relief. When she is first awakened, Lilith is served a bland, vaguely cotton-flavored mass she doesn't like. But soon she is offered bananas, pineapples, figs, nuts, bread and honey, and "a vegetable stew filled with corn, peppers, tomatoes, potatoes, onions, mushrooms, herbs, and spices," along with things like plantain, breadfruit, and "quat," a cheeselike Oankali vegetable.

Lilith and the other recently awakened humans are also surprised to discover that the Oankali—who are vegetarian and abhor bloodshed—have been trying to shape Oankali foods into forms that, at least visually, resemble foods the humans miss, like hamburgers and pie. They don't taste quite right, but it's a symbol of something, a gesture. They're trying.

But the forms these reconstructed foods take remind the humans that the Oankali are still, ultimately, in charge.

Lilith is reticent to be a part of their plan to repopulate the earth, but she slowly comes around, in part because she bonds to Nikanj, an Oankali ooloi. Ooloi, powerful healers among the Oankali, are a third gender who aid in mating and reproduction. The ooloi are vital to the Oankali plan to create "constructs," hybrid Oankali-human children whose biology will represent the best of both species, without the human contradiction's fusion of brilliance and lust for power. The humans returning to earth will be sterilized by the Oankali, making it impossible for them to reproduce on their own. They're dependent on ooloi. And Lilith is stuck in the middle of this plan.

The Oankali see their decision to sterilize humankind, to take away their ability to reproduce independently, as a noble end. They talk frequently of the human contradiction. Humans are highly intelligent, they observe, but they are "hierarchical," driven to increase their own power at the expense of others. The nuclear war (which Butler stated was inspired by the dark threat of the Cold War) was the natural result of the human contradiction. This blending of intelligence and domineering hierarchy is what makes humans who they are, and yet, the Oankali say, it's also their downfall as a species.

Even if the Oankali have rightly discerned something about humans, they're also acting with the colonizer's mindset, which Butler understood all too well. They're the powerful beings, and they're deciding the fate of the powerless. They "benevolently" bestow gifts upon the humans—healing from their frailties and diseases, a newly restored world to live on, foods that at least sometimes resemble what humans used to eat—but they're surprised when people instead want to be free from their rule, free to determine their own futures.

|||||||||||||||||||||||||||||||||

The human contradiction includes not only the juxtaposition of human ingenuity and brilliance with our lust for power and the journey to self-destruction, but also the desire to self-determine, to choose our own futures, even if it means living by our wits and scrambling for scraps. That messy reality radiates across each of Butler's science-fiction worlds, which have resonated with readers because they sense something for our time in them. It's for a similar reason that Butler's 1993 dystopian novel *Parable of the Sower* has gained popularity over the last few years (and not just because it's set in the 2020s).

In *Sower*, Lauren Oya Olamina is a woman who strikes out on her own, not fearing solitude. She lives in an America where inequality has grown so sharply that the middle class has more or less died out. Lauren's family home is in a walled community in southern California, where her father is a minister. They scrape by, but rarely venture beyond the walls of their community because the streets are dangerous. Drugs, robbery, and murder are common outside the gates.

In Lauren Olamina's world, food has grown extraordinarily expensive. She tells us a thousand dollars *might* feed her for two weeks "if I'm very careful what I buy and where I buy it. . . . Food prices are insane, always going up, never going down." It's only those who know how to forage who remain fed. Lauren loves acorn bread, made from dried and ground-up acorns, and is surprised at the idea that bread used to be made from wheat, corn, or oats, which are far too expensive now. But while people raise rabbits and chickens and gardens in their walled-off communities, desperate thieves break in and steal.

The walls aren't enough anymore. And fearing that this gated home is no longer a place of safety, Lauren decides she has to leave the community in which she grew up. She brings supplies with her, and gradually companions as well.

But her most important cargo is Earthseed, a religion she has been quietly developing through epigrammatic poems she writes in her journal. The fundamental belief of Earthseed is that God is not a being. Instead, God is change. And by participating in and directing change in the world, humans can participate in shaping God.

When Lauren begins her journey, it's because she wants to find a sustainable place for her new Earthseed community to grow food, live safely, and usher in God-shaping change. Along the road, she finds that sharing food is a way to attract people to her small band of travelers and, eventually, to her religious ideas. She signals her good will to sojourners with small gifts—shelled walnuts, apples, pomegranates, oranges, figs, bits of bread, scraps of meat—and though everyone in this dried-out land is wary of strangers, many decide to cautiously share what they have, too.

In some ways, Lauren embodies the trader tendencies of the Oankali. There's a practicality to her sharing. But in *Sower*, sharing food and eating together have an equalizing effect on the group's hierarchy. Lauren is still clearly in charge, but when they gather for a meal, the ground between her and her fellow travelers is made more level, attracting outsiders to join her community.

Growing up in a highly advanced but hideously unequal world, Lauren understands the human contradiction, the way humanity's intelligence and their compulsive need for power are always at war within them, threatening to wipe them out. That contradiction leaves people in a state of stagnation, of degeneration, unable to change the world—and that's what has destroyed her world and made it so dangerous. Lauren intuits that to overcome that contradiction and breathe new life into the world requires people to commit to a vision of a better future—not just out there, but within themselves as well. Those who wish to become members of the Earthseed community must make some essential commitments: "to learn to shape God with forethought, care, and work; to educate and benefit their community, their families, and themselves; and to contribute to the fulfillment of the Destiny." And by *Destiny* she means a purposeful life on earth, and the hope of a real heaven.

Lauren gives her followers a vision of that heaven: a peaceful life on a plot of fertile ground, where they can grow their own food, choose their own future, and nurture their Earthseed community. The Earthseed commitments, harnessing and working with change rather than rejecting it, might bring rich renewal to a species that's killing itself.

*Parable of the Sower* isn't only about a dystopian future, of course. It's also about our dystopian past. Butler was well aware of the kind of life formerly enslaved people—like Edna Lewis's or Ella Baker's grandparents—so earnestly sought as they created free communities, raised families, grew crops, slaughtered pigs, and did all they could to contribute to the fulfillment of their own destiny. Those were places of joy, but as in Lauren's world, they were also constantly aware of the threats that lay beyond their fences. With each meal, they were participating in a healing vision of equality. And they were creating a world that revolted against the human contradiction and the oppressor, at least for a while.

The world those ancestors came from is vividly illustrated in *Kindred*, perhaps Butler's best novel and one of her most haunting. Published in 1979, the book is set in the days just prior to America's bicentennial. Dana, a Black Californian writer married to a white man named Kevin, suddenly discovers herself transported, with no warning, to pre–Civil War Maryland, seemingly to save a redheaded white boy named Rufus Weylin from drowning.

Trying to figure out what has happened, Dana realizes, with a jolt, that Rufus—the son of a plantation owner—is part of her own family tree. Right now he's a boy, but soon he'll be a man. And she understands that he'll be the father of one of her own ancestors. She had known she had a relative named Rufus Weylin; she simply never knew he was white. The implications for her own parentage are disturbing, if not that surprising.

Over the course of *Kindred*, Dana finds herself flung between her own world and Rufus's. When she's in the past, time passes faster, so she sees Rufus grow into a young man. She meets Alice, the free woman he forces into slavery and into being his concubine. Eventually, Dana witnesses the birth of her own ancestor, a baby girl named Hagar.

The roles of master and enslaved person involve a profoundly hierarchical dynamic, and so food takes on a whole new meaning in *Kindred*. On Dana's third trip into the past, her husband, Kevin, finds himself dragged back in time as well, and to protect Dana from slave catchers, the plantation's sadistic overseer, and other dangers, the couple pretends that Kevin is Dana's master. As part of their cover, Dana attempts to forge a bond with the other enslaved people on the plantation, but she struggles to do so, given her odd appearance and manner of speech (she is, after all, from the future).

Even so, working in the cookhouse eventually folds her, however tenuously, into the community. She doesn't share meals with the Weylin family, who are, in a sense, her own family. The closest Dana can get to joining them at the dinner table is to serve them meals alongside the other enslaved people.

Dictating who was allowed to feast was part of how a master controlled the people they enslaved; sharing or even "trading" (in the Oankali model) would have leveled the power structure they were trying to maintain. Slavery is the ultimate expression of the human contradiction, of the drive to dominate supplanting wisdom, intelligence, and goodness. For slavery as an institution to survive, the master must deny the intelligence, and thus the humanity, of the enslaved.

But in *Kindred*, Butler takes this even further. The longer Dana is on the Weylin plantation, the more she slips into the role of an enslaved person, finding it more and more difficult to fault those who spend every day just trying to survive to the next for not attempting to escape. The extreme, abusive hierarchy, the power imbalance, the small cruelties all change the way both the powerful and the powerless view themselves. When the side of the human contradiction that lusts for power is left unchecked, it extinguishes the things that make us human.

|||||||||||||||||||||||||||||||||||||

Eating, in all of these stories, isn't rendered in sensuous detail. It is something done merely to survive. But it also tells us, quite crucially, about the cultural standing of the characters who are doing the eating, the way they relate to one another, and what a meal together extends to all of them: community, the promise of no harm, solidarity in the midst of crisis. Food, perhaps the most inescapable need humans have, more fundamental than shelter or reproduction or even freedom, can be a leveling place. When we sit at a table and, with purpose, share food that nourishes both the body and the mind, we quiet the hierarchical impulse—us over the other. And in those free places, empathy is born. For Dana in the cookhouse, Lauren on her journey, and Lilith in her quest to guide humanity in a renewed world, that lesson rings true.

Butler's life spent in "happy asociality"—which was really a life of feasting on the riches of history, science, theory, literature, and more—taught her about the human contradiction. She gained a razor-sharp understanding of what it is that threatens our life together on this planet, and she worked unceasingly to tell us stories that could serve as both bellwether and beacon, gaining recognition as both a talented writer and as someone who must be heard.

At this dinner party, listening to Butler, we can learn from her about how we can level the human contradiction when we gather together, especially when we feast. About instigating and directing change so we can keep the worst outcomes of the human contradiction at bay, and perhaps with perseverance steer ourselves away from self-destruction. About how to channel our empathy into productive avenues, and how to stop assuming that a largely solitary life can't also blossom into a fuller, wiser understanding of humanity. About grazing through the world in search of more knowledge to share. And above all, about how to live with the hope that if we simply make too much of a mess of this world, there may still be an unexpected new world, of some kind, to come.

# FEAST
## VEGETARIAN CHILI WITH WINTER SQUASH

Early in *Dawn*, Lilith is fed "a vegetable stew filled with corn, peppers, tomatoes, potatoes, onions, mushrooms, herbs, and spices," which sounds quite delicious. The Oankali are vegetarian, and so, often, are humans. But even omnivores can delight in a hearty vegetarian stew, which also turns out to be easier on earth's fragile ecosystems.

This is a slightly evolved version of my favorite vegetable chili, adapted from Martha Rose Shulman's recipe in the *New York Times*, which has many of the same ingredients as the one the Oankali gave Lilith. It is satisfying and hearty, and it has never failed to please a whole table full of eaters with every kind of dietary restriction—which, when you think about it, is a leveling of hierarchies all its own. Unlike the previous lentil soup, which makes for a lighter meal, this has chunks of squash and beans (which appear later in the *Lilith's Brood* trilogy). I can also easily imagine Lauren Olamina and the Earthseed community cooking up a pot of this if they stumbled across the right ingredients—especially when it gets colder. And it's excellent served with cornbread. (It freezes well too.)

---

3 14-oz. cans of pinto beans or about 4.5 c. of cooked pinto beans

2 T. olive oil

1 finely chopped onion

1–2 carrots, diced

1 red pepper, diced

2 cloves of garlic, minced

3 T. mild chili powder (you can, of course, go hotter if you like)

1 T. toasted cumin seeds or, if you don't have the seeds, ½ T. cumin powder (you can also use 1 T. ground coriander if you don't like or don't have cumin)

1 28-oz. can of chopped tomatoes

1 t. dried oregano

2 T. tomato paste, dissolved in 1 c. water (this is easiest if the water is hot)

1 lb. squash, whole, or 2 c. peeled, seeded, and diced. You can use basically any squash you like here; butternut is an old standby, but I've made this with carnival squash, which was festive and delicious. Acorn would be great too.

Salt

½ c. cilantro for garnish, if you like

Grated cheese, to sprinkle on top, if desired

---

## Optional Oankali Additions

1 c. fresh or frozen corn kernels

2 diced potatoes

1 c. diced mushrooms, probably big portobellos, as they'll hold up best in soup and provide a kind of meat texture for the omnivores at your party (my husband swears by them for this recipe).

---

1. If using diced squash, skip to step 3. If using whole squash, heat your oven to 400 degrees. Prick the squash all over with a fork as best you can—it will be quite hard. When the oven is heated, put the squash on a sheet pan or in a baking dish and roast for around 40 minutes, until you can prick it and it's not hard anymore. You want it to be easy to cut into, but not completely done, because you're going to dice it instead of mashing it.

2. Remove the squash, let it cool, then cut it in half and peel it. (You may be able to peel the skin right off like paper, depending on the variety; otherwise, slice it off with a knife.) Seed it, then cut into small chunks, at a size that looks comfortable to put into your mouth. You could do all of this without roasting it, but it's much easier once roasted. Your goal is to have a pile of slightly roasted squash chunks, about 2 cups' worth, though more or less won't hurt.

3. Put the beans into a big pot on your stovetop, over medium-high heat, with some water or vegetable broth if necessary to keep them from burning. Don't skimp on the size of the pot. You're going to be adding a lot of yummy goodness to it.

4. In a large skillet, preferably nonstick, heat the oil over medium-high heat. (You can do this in a ceramic dutch oven if you prefer, or cast-iron.) Add the onion, carrot, and pepper; if you're using mushrooms, add them now. Cook for about 8 minutes, until it starts to smell good.

5. Add the garlic and stir everything together for about a minute, then add the cumin and chili powder.

Cook for about 2–3 minutes; the mixture should start to stick to the pan.

6. Dump in the tomatoes, salt, and oregano, and bring it to a simmer. Cook for about 10 minutes, till everything starts to get thick and seems like it's beginning to stick to the pan again. Stir in the tomato paste and bring it back to a simmer, add some salt, and cook for another 10 minutes. It should smell delicious.

7. Pour the entire tomato mixture into the pot of beans, and if you're using potatoes or corn, add them now. Next, add the diced squash to the pot. Bring the whole thing to a simmer, and cook for 30–45 minutes. Stir frequently to keep it from burning, and add a little broth or water if it seems like it's getting too thick or if you just want it a little more soupy. You'll know the chili is done when you can poke a piece of winter squash (and a potato, if you're using potatoes) with a fork and the tines go right through it.

8. Once you're satisfied that it's fully cooked, taste it, and add additional salt if needed. (You can add pepper if you like.)

9. Serve it in bowls as is, or top with cheese (or the Oankali fictional cheese-like fruit, quat, I suppose, which may just mean cashew cheese on our planet) and cilantro. You could also garnish it with croutons, or crushed tortilla chips, or sour cream, or Greek yogurt. This is a flexible and hearty stew, and you can put the leftovers in the freezer for

several weeks, or the refrigerator for four or five days, though it's probably still fine after a week. (Use your nose and tongue, like Varda's gleaners, to confirm.) Share it with your friends and neighbors. Trade it, even. And let it level your dinner-table hierarchies.

# More Salt with Octavia Butler

*Kindred*, the *Lilith's Brood* trilogy (*Dawn*, *Adulthood Rites*, and *Imago*), and *Parable of the Sower*: Among her most vital novels; they're all worthy of reading, but start here.

*A Handful of Earth, a Handful of Sky: The World of Octavia Butler*, by Lynell George: A visually rich plunge into the marginalia and ephemera that Butler left behind—including photographs, notes to herself, ticket stubs, and copies of receipts—and the story they tell about her life. It's like a biography birthed from a scrapbook.

*Conversations with Octavia Butler*, edited by Consuela Francis: An anthology of decades of interviews with Butler. It paints a picture of the author's evolving lines of thought and helps readers recognize her recurring themes. In each interview, Butler's winsome, hospitable, and concise thinking sparkles.

"How Octavia E. Butler Reimagines Sex and Survival," by Julian Lucas, in the *New Yorker*'s March 15, 2021, issue: An exceptional overview of Butler's work and its continued importance, particularly on what she envisioned as the goal of living.

HANNAH ARENDT

## CHAPTER SEVEN

# HANNAH ARENDT
## THE SUBVERSIVE FEAST OF FRIENDS

Imagine it: New York City. The 1950s. An apartment building on Riverside Drive. Even before you reach the door, you can hear the buzzing, a clamoring hum punctuated by laughter. The heavy door pushes open, someone takes your coat, and now you're inside. A dozen people sit in the living room, palming tumblers and martini glasses, alternating sips with a drag off their cigarette, untidy little heaps of smoldering butts in the ashtrays around the room telling you these friends have been here a while. As the sun sets over the Hudson, there's no cocktail party small talk; they are shouting with passion—though, you notice, no aggression or malice. The topic becomes briefly unintelligible as some slip into German and then, after glancing around the room at those who've fallen silent, back into English.

Books shoved into cases ring the room around the tweed-clad group, mostly men, mostly bespectacled, mostly recognizable from the lecture halls and barrooms and magazine offices around town, and in the middle of them all sits one woman with short, unmanageable hair and a wise smile: Hannah Arendt. This is her home. And this is the only place in the city you'd want to be.

The setting changed frequently, but from the 1940s to the 1960s, most weeks you could find a similar scene somewhere in New York. It was a recurring reincarnation of a tradition stretching back a century or more, to the European salons run by women, often Jewish women, with a keen interest in ideas, art, and people. This moveable feast went on for decades, with new faces, new concerns, but always the same goals: to find oneself among friends or frenemies, lovers and former lovers, colleagues and cordial nemeses, and hash out what was going on in the world while nourishing the soul (and the stomach, too).

This salon was made up of a group that historians would one day call the New York Intellectuals. Many were Jewish émigrés from Europe or American Jews. All of them wanted to understand the most fundamental things about life in a world that felt as if it had gone mad. They had been influential since the 1930s, growing in number as they wrote in journals mostly to and about one another, a loud dinner party conducted in pages so everyone could eavesdrop. But they'd found themselves living on unstable ground. Only recently had the full horrors of Hitler's Holocaust become known to the public. For a lot of the New York Intellectuals, the discovery felt like it split history in two. Basic assumptions about humanity, about what people are and are not capable of, disappeared beneath the shadow of millions of dead souls. And they were growing ever more certain that the future depended on their ability to come to terms with the past.

No one was more aware of this than Arendt. A brilliant German Jewish woman, a philosopher by training, who had fled her homeland in 1941 and a few years later was publishing (in her third language, English) in journals like *Partisan Review* and *Commentary*, she knew what was at stake. In 1951, she published a hefty book, *The Origins of Totalitarianism*, which traced the roots of what was happening in Europe, from Nazism to Stalinism. In it, she wrote about what led to the rise of totalizing power, which erases people's humanity by erasing their individuality. Totalitarianism tries to deny both individual citizens' uniqueness and their ability to act collectively against systems of oppression. And most of all, it makes impossible what Arendt says makes us human, and what was happening in that apartment over cocktails: the all-important act of *thinking*.

The enormity of what happened in Germany and across Europe, the horrors from which she and her Berliner husband Heinrich Blücher fled, appear out of place amid the merry, impassioned band of drinkers feasting on ideas and canapés in Arendt's apartment. But reading between the lines of Arendt's work from *The Origins of Totalitarianism* onward, you can see why this group of intellectuals mattered to her. They helped her think, but they also modeled a crucial concept: revolutions may be happening all over the world, but right here, in this little group, in this little apartment, a small revolution was happening, too.

Let's level on one thing: Strictly speaking, a cocktail party is not a feast, or even a dinner party. It's a different kind of production—it's theater. "Cocktail party chatter" is the phrase we use to denote conversation that's shallowly performative. A cocktail party is where you go to see and be seen, to catch someone's eye, to impress, to make an appearance and get pleasantly buzzed (or embarrassingly drunk) before you saunter home or repair to a nearby restaurant for an actual meal. Most of the time, a cocktail party is a stage, not an evocation of home. And that, friends, can get tiring.

But while Arendt and her circle did all of those things at their parties, there was something else unfolding there, too—something feast-ly. Sure, they came to gossip. They came to be seen, to engage in intrigue, to quarrel, to flirt, to test out new members of the group so they could laugh about them later. They drank, and sometimes they'd eat too, but the main thing they took in was talk.

And it wasn't empty or small talk. In fact, I bet their lack of small talk was a point of pride among them. Their cocktail parties became legendary not because of their extravagance or their spectacle, but because they were where the group thought together, as friends. For them, arguing was a way in which to build a world and test out ideas on one another. These gatherings were a boozy still point in a world spinning off its axis. If an idea appeared in *Partisan Review* or *Commentary* or the *New Yorker*, or in a book that set the intellectual world ablaze, or ricocheted around a classroom at Bard or Columbia or Berkeley, it might have first been hashed out and honed over some very stiff martinis on Riverside Drive.

I don't mean to romanticize these parties—though they've enchanted me since I first read about them years ago, and I've tried to recreate them sometimes, too; they're the measuring stick by which I judge my own soirées. The New York Intellectuals' gatherings, even the most intimate ones, had more than their fair share of bad fights and sneering posers. Friendships fell apart, appalling ideas were floated, hangovers were renewed, and a lot of questionable behavior transpired. (Just read their letters and diaries.)

But there was something fundamentally solid and generative about their gatherings. We're still talking about them, after all—not just the parties, but the people, and their ideas. And when you look at Hannah Arendt's writing, you can clearly see that these cocktail parties were a key part to her understanding of how the forces that wanted to eradicate the humanness of humanity—forces she understood all too well—could be defeated at their own game.

||||||||||||||||||||||||||||||

To distill Hannah Arendt's philosophy and history into bite-sized helpings is impossible. She wrote reams. She presented lectures and gave talks. Her ideas were always evolving, because she was always having conversations with friends and with herself. To Arendt, "thinking" is best understood as a conversation with the self.

By the time Arendt was famous, she'd come to believe that the project of life wasn't to think about the world's problems in order to solve them, since no single fix could be found. Instead, the goal was to keep *thinking*. After *The Origins of Totalitarianism*, she wrote other books that made big waves, among them her 1958 magnum opus, *The Human Condition*, and her 1963 book, *Eichmann in Jerusalem: A Report on the Banality of Evil*, which began as a series in the *New Yorker* and landed her in the middle of a cultural firestorm with those who objected to her characterization of its subject, Adolf Eichmann, a primary architect of the Final Solution.

In the ensuing years, she has continued to be a figure worth arguing with, which is just as she would have wanted. Arendt's work is both highly personal and entirely impersonal. You come away from her writing understanding what she thinks, but only having a vague sense of who she really was. Her work is animated by a voice that's often wry, even funny, and frequently scathingly angry; she was not a philosopher who lived detached from the world. What happened to other people mattered to her.

But you wouldn't necessarily know from her books and essays that she lived on Riverside Drive, or maintained a tight circle of friends, or that she smoked like a chimney. She writes with a strong voice, but rarely in the first person. And yet, her clear, cogent point of view gives you a picture of Hannah, the person, and what mattered to her.

Like most great writers, Hannah Arendt wrote about the same few topics over and over, refashioned and reconfigured to fit new circumstances. Maybe her most important recurring idea is *amor mundi*—the love of the world. (She intended to use the phrase as the title for the book she eventually named *The Human Condition*.) *Amor mundi* was not a rosy slogan to slap on a plaque or repeat as a mantra. It's not her "Live Laugh Love"-style motto. For Arendt, *amor mundi* had a very specific meaning, with responsibilities attached to it.

Arendt's concept of what *love* means is multifaceted, influenced strongly by her 1929 dissertation, which she titled *Der Liebesbegriff bei Augustin* (*Love and St. Augustine*). Augustine is a central voice in Christian history and thought, so he could seem like an odd choice for Arendt, who was Jewish and not particularly observant. And yet she both quarrels with and adopts parts of Christian theology in her writing. Her focus on the true meaning of "loving the world" was likely in reaction to what was happening around her. She saw Christianity as tumbling toward a dislocated "unworldliness"—encouraging the faithful to turn their eyes away from the world in order to love God. Teachings like those, she felt, lead people to effect evil on earth in the name of God.

A Jewish woman like Arendt, who was forced to flee her homeland because most Christians there simply complied with the evils of the Third Reich, had plenty of reasons to question what Christianity means when it talks about love. And the root of the evil she had to flee, as Arendt would later write, came from a culture, a people, who at best refused to think. They were too busy protecting and advancing their own well-being and power to protect the powerless and those in need. That's the root of evil.

Yet to Arendt, loving the world doesn't mean being "in love" with it. Nor does it mean fooling yourself about the world and closing your eyes to the realities of history and injustice.

Instead, as she argued and wrote about it, loving the world means working on two specific tasks. The first is to doggedly insist on seeing the world just as it is, with its disappointments and horrors—and committing to it all the same. The second is to encounter people in the world and embrace their *alterity*, or difference.

That last piece—loving people for their difference—is essential to Arendt's thinking, as well as her social gatherings. She emphasized that we are each profoundly unique. The world is made up of individual people, with individual characteristics. It is individuals, in our "plurality," who make up a society. And so, that society can never be perfect.

But part of true *amor mundi* is the recognition that our problems will never be fixed, that there is no perfect theory or principle that will unlock the puzzle of existence and solve our problems. And, Arendt writes, that's why politics exists. In politics, we come together, committed to the world, willing to raise our eyes and look at one another, to debate and critically discuss the world, continually working our way toward what we would like it to become, knowing the work will never be "finished." Doing so requires us to see one another as individuals with equal dignity but very different ways of being. It is our idiosyncrasies that make us who we are, and it is those unique traits and eccentricities that empower us to care for one another. We see how someone is different from us, and we choose to love that difference, thus expanding our love beyond ourselves.

Arendt took some heat for saying that it's impossible to "love" people in the abstract. She argued that she couldn't declare love for categories of people—Jews, she said, or women—because to love someone, you have to know them, in all of their distinctive individuality. "The moment we want to say who somebody is, our very vocabulary leads us astray into saying what he is," she wrote in *The Human Condition.* You could *care* for people because they were human; you could fight for them, create organizations to protect them, write columns to defend them, and put your body on the line for them. But you could only *love* individual people. When you love a person, what you love is all the ways they are different from everyone else. To put it another way, what makes me *me* is all the ways I am not you, or anyone else. And so, if you love me, that is what you love: the very particular mix of things that together constitute me. You can respect the what, but you can only love the who.

So, politics is where we focus on everything that happens between all the individuals who make up a society. It's where we repair the threads that bind us together. We can only do this if we acknowledge what has happened in the past and look closely at the present. We must understand that people see the world differently for different reasons, but we can't make up stories that paper over our reality. Racial history, class oppression, gender discrimination, prejudices of all kinds—we have to own up to them all. That's how we start to generate freedom.

But that requires us to think and talk with others—and sometimes drink and eat with them, too. We must gather over cocktails to bounce our perspectives off of one another and tangle with them directly if we are to truly understand and love the world. Otherwise, how can one person, in their specificity, grasp the enormity of history and existence?

There's a problem, of course. Just looking at the world reveals it's a mess. Arendt described it as living in "desert" conditions— we are dropped down into a broken world, where humans hurt one another. To love the world, we need "oases" where we can retreat and be renewed. Those oases include art and music and poetry and dinner tables and cocktail parties and, perhaps most importantly, friendship.

That's why friendship is everything to Arendt. It is the strongest of the oases, the one that keeps us from turning inward on ourselves and away from the horrors of the world. It is where we learn to appreciate others not for the ways they are the same as us, but for how they're different from us. It is where we overcome the horror of isolation, but also avoid becoming just another face in the crowd, lost in the collective. Friendship is the connective tissue that builds us into a true society and saves us from being overtaken by totalitarianism.

"Arendt sees friendship as allied to politics: not as a substitute for politics, nor as a way of doing politics, but as a condition necessary for the survival of politics as she understood it," writes Jon Nixon in his book *Hannah Arendt and the Politics of Friendship.* "Friendship is what lies between the private world of the familial, tribal, and religious affiliation, and the political world of institutional and association affiliation based not on family, tribe, or religion but on equality."

In our polarized age, the idea of friendship being necessary for politics is strange to ponder. (It probably felt the same to her contemporaries.) But for Arendt, politics was not an all-encompassing identity marker. Just as importantly, she wasn't saying that friendship with people "across the aisle" is somehow going to save us.

Instead Arendt means something slightly different: that friendship with other people (including those you generally agree with) subverts power. Friendship—in which people see and recognize one another's differences, affirm and challenge those differences, and ultimately grow—pushes back against tyrannical forces that try to deny our individuality and dignity. Friends don't become more like one another; instead, as Nixon puts it, "through our friendships we learn to relate to one another as free and equal agents and, crucially, to carry what we have learned from those friendships—by way of the exercise of freedom and the recognition of equal worth—back into the world."

Arendt famously poured herself into making and maintaining friendships—even with people whom she might reasonably have been expected to abandon over her life. Her most strange and even uncomfortable friendship was with the philosopher Martin Heidegger, her former professor and, some believe, the great love of her life. They conducted a passionate, clandestine affair for a couple of years, beginning when he was thirty-five and she was eighteen (and still his student). The relationship waned after Arendt left town to study with Karl Jaspers (who would ultimately become an even more valuable mentor for her). Heidegger then joined the Nazi Party, apparently enthusiastically. In spite of this fact, in the years following the war, Arendt—now married to Blücher and living in New York—tried to reestablish contact, and for her whole life would doggedly pursue a friendship with Heidegger, seeing him as a profitable intellectual partner, if not a romantic one. By all accounts he was, it seems, a rather exasperating man to befriend. But even if Arendt could not always provoke the kind of engagement she craved, she found him to still be worth her time; you can detect her quarreling with Heidegger in her later work, particularly in her idea that there is no one philosophical key that will unlock the mystery of existence (as he believed death was). Life, for Arendt, is something we must continually wrestle with.

A much more satisfying friendship came in the form of Mary McCarthy, the writer and critic, though the friendship was almost ruined from the start. They first met in 1944, on one hazy Manhattan night in a bar. They'd both been brought there by friends—McCarthy by the art critic Clement Greenberg, with whom she was having an anemic affair, and Arendt by Greenberg's brother Martin, her coworker at Schocken Books, where she was working as a secretary. McCarthy (married at the time to the critic Edmund Wilson) already had made her reputation. Arendt was still new to New York and was just beginning to publish in some of the most incisive, radical journals headquartered there: *Partisan Review*, *The Nation*, *Commentary*.

Decades later, McCarthy told Carol Brightman, who edited a collection of letters between the pair, that she recalled Arendt having an "extraordinary electric vitality" that filled her "with delight and wonder" that night at the bar. Imagine the scene from McCarthy's point of view: dim lighting, wood-paneled walls, the men in their suits, and then this thirtysomething European stranger, sitting across the table, waving her cigarette around, uncowed by the fact that she was a stranger to the group. That night, Arendt talked animatedly about the United States, how it was still malleable and unfinished compared to her native Germany, a young country finding its footing. That kind of force would appeal to McCarthy, a woman who had built her life on having an opinion and stating it boldly, but with charm.

Oddly, the pair didn't become friends that night. In fact, the next recorded interaction between them, in 1945, was an outright disaster. They were at—what else?—a cocktail party, and McCarthy made a crack about Hitler calculated to scandalize her more sanctimonious liberal friends. She expressed that she felt sorry for Hitler, an absurd man who wanted his victims to love him. Arendt was incensed. "How can you say such a thing in front of me—a victim of Hitler, a person who has been in a concentration camp!" she exclaimed, and then stormed out. Any chance of a relationship between the two seemed impossible.

But in the airtight, insular world of their intellectual circle, with mutual friends and mutual interests, they inevitably kept crossing paths. One night, after they both attended a gathering, they ended up standing on the same subway platform, no doubt waiting for one of those interminably delayed late-night trains that make you feel suspended in time, especially when you've had a bit of gin. Each had found in debates that they were frequently on the same side against the rest of the room. "Let's end this nonsense," Arendt finally said to McCarthy, breaking a three-year silence. "We think so much alike." They made amends. And thus a friendship was born that would last the rest of their lives.

If you read their letters, you get to see the true Arendt. She is funny, confident, encouraging to her friend. She likes food and travel and cities and people, and she willingly gives advice about love to McCarthy—who went through many affairs and two marriages during their friendship—and seeks her perspective on the current discourse around ideas like freedom and tyranny. She invites her to stay the night at her apartment in New York frequently, and they are always orbiting one another, aware of where the other is and what they are doing, wherever they are in the world. Their flinty intellects show a soft side for one another, in spite of their differences.

That relationship, assiduously maintained by the pair until Arendt passed away in 1975—after which McCarthy put aside her own work to prepare Arendt's unfinished book, *The Life of the Mind*, for publication—is an ideal model for what Arendt thought friendship could do. Friendship is a place for public happiness, a give-and-take that is receptive to the world and to others. So friendship is revolutionary. It confronts and rebukes totalitarianism. Thinking and sharpening one another helps stave off evil; in friendship, we encourage one another to think. "It is within that place—the place of friendship—that friends are able to explore the truth of their opinions by 'talking things over' and through the 'give and take' of conviviality," Nixon writes. Friendship in Arendt's thinking, he later notes, is a "microcosm of the polity—not seeking to replace or juxtapose itself against the polity, but sustaining and modeling it."

I learn from Hannah Arendt that a feast is only possible among friends, or people whose hearts are open to becoming friends. Or you could put it another way: any meal can become a feast when shared with friends engaged in the activity of thinking their way through the world and loving it together.

Arendt rarely wrote about food itself except as sustenance, but her life and love of being with friends over drinks and meals suggests she knew what is worth knowing. A mere meal is a necessity for life, a fact of being human. But it is transformed into something much more important, something vital to the life of the world, when the people who share the table are engaging in the practices of love and of thinking.

Personally, I've gotten tired of performative cocktail parties. Mostly, I skip them. In the early days of the pandemic, cocktail parties moved online, with everyone bringing their own drink and sitting at a screen. And that seemed even worse. But then, one late summer night, four friends from graduate school arranged for us to catch up over drinks—I made a stiff Gibson martini, and then another—and we talked about everything: new jobs, houses, the people we used to know, what we thought of ideas we'd been reading, the things we were worried about, the new baby two of them had just had. We sat there for hours, until it became too late (at least in my time zone) for me to stay up any longer. It was not a feast, in a technical sense—not like any feast we'd shared in the past, where we ate and drank and got a little silly.

But it felt like a feast regardless. And now I know why: Together, through the staying power of our long friendship, we are learning to love the world and one another in our particularities, and in that is something no power can overcome.

# FEAST
## A STIFF GIBSON

The twist that makes a martini a Gibson is the onion. I don't have any idea if anyone in Hannah Arendt's circle loved a Gibson, but I know for certain they enjoyed their martinis. There are many ways to make a martini: with vodka or gin (which come in many varieties), with lots of vermouth or only a whisper of it, with lemon twists or olives, and the list goes on.

Instead of trying to be historically accurate, I'm simply going to give you my favorite recipe for a martini, the way I make it for myself when I'm at home. It is absolutely not to everyone's taste, but it's very much to mine. Love me in my particularity.

---

2 ½ oz. gin, or to be honest, probably 3 oz. (I like Hendrick's if I'm at a bar or, for a visually stunning treat, Empress 1908 Indigo Gin.)

Dry vermouth (preferably Dolin or Carpano Dry)

3 cocktail onions (Sable and Rosenfeld if you like them sweet, but my favorite are made by Filthy Food—tart and with a pleasingly acidic bite)

---

1. To avoid using a cocktail shaker, I use a cavernous, stemless wine glass. Pour just a dash of dry vermouth into the glass, barely more than a rinse.

2. Place the largest ice cube you can find into the glass if you're using one that can accommodate it; otherwise put it into a cocktail shaker. Pour the gin on top of the ice. Using a cocktail spoon, or just the narrowest spoon you can find, stir for 30 seconds,

until you can feel how cold the gin has gotten through the glass. (Absolutely do *not* shake it—that creates ice shards in your drink. James Bond was wrong.)

3. You can take the ice cube out, or leave it in if you want; it will water down the drink over time, but if you're planning a long night of debating with friends, a little hydration in the second half of your drink might be for the best.

4. Put two or three cocktail onions on a cocktail pick or a long toothpick—that way you don't have to fish around for them later, and you can enjoy nibbling on them between sips (the best part!).

5. That's it. Drink up. And if you want to remember tonight tomorrow, have a glass of water before you mix another.

Alongside a good martini, I like salty breadsticks, or popcorn sprinkled with garlic salt, but any manner of canapés would work. Or pair with one of my late-night snacks: open a tin of anchovy fillets and use a toothpick to fish (heh) them out to eat one at a time. Eat them on top of the saltiest potato chips you can find. *Amor mundi*, indeed.

# MORE SALT WITH HANNAH ARENDT

*The Three Escapes of Hannah Arendt: A Tyranny of Truth*, by Ken Krimstein: A rich, engrossing biography of Arendt, told in graphic-novel form, that's a great introduction to her world.

*Hannah Arendt and the Politics of Friendship*, by Jon Nixon: A short study of Arendt's views on friendship, with chapters on four of her most important friendships as illustrations.

*Hannah Arendt: For the Love of the World*, by Elizabeth Young-Bruehl: A comprehensive and, more importantly, readable biography. It's loaded with stories, letters, books, and other primary sources that truly round out Arendt's character.

*The Origins of Totalitarianism* and *The Human Condition*: Arendt's two most well-known books, and both relatively accessible to those new to her thought.

*Hannah Arendt*, directed by Margarethe von Trotta: An engaging 2012 film about Arendt during the period in which she wrote *Eichmann in Jerusalem*. Thankfully, it includes lots of cocktail parties.

## CHAPTER EIGHT

# ALICE B. TOKLAS
## LET ME BE AN ARTIST

Imagine waking up one day and casually making lunch for the world's most influential painters and writers. Imagine they're your friends, they live not far down a tangled web of Parisian streets, and they pop by for lunch all the time. Imagine you have a trove of Matisse and Cézanne paintings in your home, hung in a room where artists often gather to discuss art and life. Just imagine.

That was Alice B. Toklas's life. And in the cookbook she published in 1954, long after those meals had passed into memory, she wrote about one such memorable lunch with her old friend Pablo Picasso.

The painter had come to the apartment Toklas shared with Gertrude Stein, her lifelong partner, whom she met on her first day in Paris in 1907. Toklas doesn't say exactly when this lunch took place; perhaps she didn't remember. But throughout her life with Stein, Toklas managed the household and did much of the cooking, and that day, she decided to serve a striped bass. She poached it in some dry white wine with various herbs and vegetables. And then, on a whim, she decided to decorate it—"in a way that I thought would amuse him," she writes. After the fish cooled, she drained it, set it on a platter, and got to work:

> A short time before serving it I covered the fish with an ordinary mayonnaise and, using a pastry tube, decorated it with a red mayonnaise, not coloured with catsup—horror of horrors—but with tomato paste. Then I made a design with sieved hard-boiled eggs, the whites and the yolks apart, with truffles and with finely chopped *fines herbes*. I was proud of my *chef d'oeuvre* when it was served and Picasso exclaimed at its beauty. But, said he, should it not rather have been made in honor of Matisse than of me.

Picasso was not wrong; the bright reds and yellows probably resembled Henri Matisse's vivid paintings more than his own work. But the memory stuck with Toklas for decades, a proud moment worth recounting in writing. She wanted to remember the fish.

And she wanted to remember a lot more, too. *The Alice B. Toklas Cook Book* may advertise itself as a collection of recipes by a woman whose name was so recognizable when it came out that she might be called a celebrity. But it reads more like a memoir than a "cook book," full of stories about her life with Stein (whom she always refers to by her full name, "Gertrude Stein"), and friends, and friends of friends, and quirky household help, and years spent trying to outlive wars. It's cheerful, and often very funny. But there's an undeniable wistfulness to it, too—a need to preserve what had passed, lest it disappear entirely.

After reading similarly memory-laden cookbooks by Edna Lewis and Elizabeth David and Laurie Colwin, Toklas's approach feels familiar. But if the techniques are similar, the aims are different. In Lewis's books, she recounts her childhood and amends deficient narratives in American history. Colwin's stories urge readers to let their hair down, take big risks, and have fun in the kitchen. And David, through her "dirty words," her memories of eating bright and fresh food during dark days, managed to bring whole new culinary horizons into existence.

Toklas's cookbook manages to do all of these things at times. She even includes a chapter on seven kinds of cold vegetable soup from southern regions of Europe, each of which she thinks may be related to the others—a move that could have been lifted straight from David's playbook.

But though Toklas's chief aim is to introduce her readers to French cooking, she ends up doing something else entirely. In fact, *The Alice B. Toklas Cook Book* pulls off two things equally well. It takes the extraordinary life that she and Stein lived together and turns it into a sensory journey. And, even more crucially, it makes us feel that cooking is not just about food—it's an art form, one worth serious attention and boundless creativity, because food is the visceral anchor for all of our memories.

iiiiiiiiiiiiiiiiiiiiiiiiiiiiii

In 1906, a catastrophic earthquake rocked San Francisco, where twenty-nine-year-old Alice Toklas lived and had, in part, grown up. She was musical, educated, and relatively well-off. Her mother had died nearly ten years earlier, at which point Toklas took over as housekeeper for her father and younger brother. Now she was nearing thirty and increasingly certain she'd never marry or live the traditional life that was expected of a woman of her class and age; she had come to realize that she was attracted to women, and at the turn of the century that meant always being an outsider.

After the earthquake, Toklas met Michael Stein and his wife Sarah, who were visiting from their home in Paris. The couple had traveled to San Francisco to check on their family properties and assess the damage. When Toklas heard their stories of life abroad, she knew she simply had to go there, at least to visit. It sounded like somewhere she might belong.

The following year, accompanied by her friend Harriet Levy, Toklas made it to Paris, where she met Gertrude Stein, Michael's sister. The rest is history.

At the time, Gertrude—highly educated and marvelously ambitious, always hoping to overturn the world with her experimental writing—was living with her brother Leo. Their flat was located at 27 rue de Fleurus, an address that would soon become famous among artists, writers, and intellectuals. Using money from their family trust, the whole family collected art. But Gertrude and Leo's collection would soon be the more prestigious of the group. They had begun collecting art from painters they found interesting, some of whom were already famous and some of whom were still on their way to becoming the recognized masters they are today. Paintings by Renoir, Gauguin, Cézanne, and Delacroix were among the early works they bought. Eventually, Picasso was added to the collection, and in 1906, he completed a famous portrait of Gertrude Stein. (It now hangs in New York's Metropolitan Museum of Art.)

By the time Toklas came to see the Steins in Paris, the studio at 27 rue de Fleurus was full of art's greatest hits. So, not long after their own introduction, Gertrude Stein was introducing Toklas to Picasso at his studio, where he was working on *Les Demoiselles d'Avignon*, which would cause a ruckus in the art world when it was exhibited later that year, though eventually it would become one of the most influential paintings in modern art.

Toklas and Stein quickly bonded, taking long walks during which they'd talk about Stein's writing. After a summer with friends in Italy in 1908, Toklas became Stein's editor, typist, and secretary. Stein claimed she couldn't start writing until 11:00 p.m., when she could be sure nobody would stop by to see the art. So each morning, Toklas would collect Stein's pages from the night before, decipher them, and type them up before Stein rose around noon.

During this time, Toklas had been living with her friend Harriet Levy around the corner, on rue Notre Dame des Champs. But in 1910, she moved in with Gertrude and Leo. Toklas would often make their meals when the cook they employed had the night off. The historian Wanda Corn, a scholar of Gertrude Stein, noted how important eating and cooking were to their relationship right from the start. "Alice would make American food for Gertrude, which she was feeling a little nostalgic for," Corn told *Smithsonian* magazine. And when it came to the kitchen, "Alice was also a really demanding supervisor of the cook. Shopping had to be done 'just so' and at the very right places, veggies had to all be picked that morning. It was the one room, she said, where nobody else was allowed."

In the *Cook Book*, Toklas writes that while she was in San Francisco, keeping house for her family, she really wasn't interested in cooking. But when she moved in with the Steins, Toklas states, Gertrude "said we would have American food for Sunday-evening supper, she had had enough French and Italian cooking; the servant would be out and I should have the kitchen to myself." So Toklas started making foods she remembered from California's San Joaquin Valley: "fricasseed chicken, corn bread, apple and lemon pie."

Eventually she learned to cook all kinds of cuisines, in part from observing the rotating cast of characters who worked as cooks in her kitchen. An entire chapter of the *Cook Book* is devoted to the foibles, follies, and triumphs of their various cooks, some of whom were much better than others. But when they didn't or couldn't have a cook, the job fell to Toklas, who seemed to utterly delight in it. Stein encouraged her to find creative joy in the kitchen, and she did.

It helped that they were in France where, as Toklas wrote, their approach to food is notable. Americans living in France would write about French culinary culture repeatedly throughout the twentieth century—people like Julia Child, James Beard, and M.F.K. Fisher (who wrote an exuberant preface to the 1984 edition of Toklas's book). Formal French cooking, they'd all note, has strict rules and traditions, but there's also a rich variety of cuisines available across the country, and an inherent interest in good, fresh food. It felt different from what people were eating in America.

Toklas, though, takes it one step further, comparing the French appreciation for meals to their national interest in the fine arts. In lines reminiscent of Elizabeth David, she writes that the French "bring to their consideration of the table the same appreciation, respect, intelligence, and lively interest that they have for the other arts, for painting, for literature and for the theatre." Although the observation is obviously inflected by years spent living among a certain class and social set in Paris, she is onto something: culinary pursuits are an art form like any other, and the sustenance they provide is not purely measured in calories and nutrients. Like all art, a good meal feeds the mind and soul as well as the body. Thus, it's as worthy of conversation and attention as a painting or piece of music, or a novel or play.

Toklas also noted that "conversation even in a literary or political *salon* can turn to the subject of menus, food or wine." She would know. The Saturday night salon at the flat on rue de Fleurus was already the stuff of legends. Friends would bring their own friends, and when the so-called "Lost Generation" eventually arrived in Paris—mostly Americans, like Hemingway, who came of age during World War I—they were drawn to Stein and Toklas and their famous salon, too. (Stein is also widely credited with dubbing those gifted young people, mostly men, with that moniker.) The *New York Times* obituary for Toklas lists some of the attendees at the Stein and Toklas salons:

> At their Paris homes they gathered a dazzling array of the famous, the ambitious, the wealthy and the curious—Ernest Hemingway, Carl Van Vechten, T.S. Eliot, Alfred North Whitehead, F. Scott Fitzgerald, Thornton Wilder, Picasso, Matisse, Gris, Braque, Virgil Thomson, Charles Chaplin, Sherwood Anderson, Glenway Wescott, Paul Robeson, Jo Davidson, Pavel Tchelichev, Ford Maddox Ford and Richard Wright, to name some.

It was a formidable crowd, and Stein reigned at the center of it. Biographers note that Toklas spent time with the "geniuses' wives" rather than with the geniuses, who crowded around Stein. In fact, Stein makes a wry joke about it in her book *The Autobiography of Alice B. Toklas*, which Stein wrote in an accessible version of her own modernist style, and yet authored in Toklas's voice:

> Before I decided to write this book [*sic*] my twenty-five years with Gertrude Stein, I had often said that I would write, The wives of geniuses I have sat with. I have sat with so many. I have sat with wives who were not wives, of geniuses who were real geniuses. I have sat with real wives of geniuses who were not real geniuses. I have sat with wives of geniuses, of near geniuses, of would be geniuses, in short I have sat very often and very long with many wives and wives of many geniuses.

Every Saturday night, their salons were a feast—of ideas and art, friends and foes, love and beauty, fights and drama, and so much shouting. Life in Paris before and between the wars was heady and brilliant. Stein and Toklas's crowd was staid compared to what you might find in the more bohemian corners of Montmartre. But these gatherings were vital to the development of modernism, and it's hard to say what the world of art would have looked like without them.

Beloved of historians though they may be, the salons are not the focus of Toklas's cookbook. She spends more time recounting the meals they had at other people's houses, the travels she and Stein took together, and, for a long stretch, the challenges of living with dignity and not too much deprivation when France was occupied during the war—years she and Stein spent mostly in the countryside. Toklas saw their "American ingenuity" as a boon during this time: "We found combinations and replacements which pointed in new directions and created a fresh and absorbing interest in everything pertaining to the kitchen." Meanwhile, the French suffered from lack of access to the ingredients that were central to traditional French cooking. Toklas claimed in the 1950s that they'd still not recovered:

> Wars change the way of life, habits, markets and so eventually cooking. For five years and more the French were deprived of most of their foodstuffs and were obliged to use inferior substitutes when they could be found. After the Liberation the markets very slowly were supplied with a limited amount of material. The population had been hungry too long, they had lost their old disciplined appreciation of food and had forgotten or were ignoring their former critical judgment. So that even now French food has not yet returned to its old standard.

"Things used to be better" is a familiar sentiment, and usually it makes me sigh with frustration when I run across it; nostalgia for some golden past is a fiction that filters down to readers through rosy spectacles. But in Toklas's case the feeling was personal. By the time she wrote *The Alice B. Toklas Cook Book*, she was approaching her eighties, struggling with illness, and alone—Stein had passed away in 1946. Since at the time they couldn't legally marry, Toklas had no claim to Stein's impressive art collection or wealth; Stein had tried to ensure that the paintings would remain with Toklas until she too died, but the family pilfered them from her apartment when she was out of town. During her final years, Toklas was supported only by the generosity of friends, until she died in 1967.

When Toklas wrote *The Alice B. Toklas Cook Book*, she was on bed rest. "I must confide that this book with its mingling of recipe and reminiscence was put together during the first three months of an attack of pernicious jaundice," she writes in the foreword. "Partly, I suppose, it was written as an escape from the narrow diet and monotony of illness, and I daresay nostalgia for old days and old ways and for remembered health and enjoyment lent special lustre to dishes and menus barred from an invalid table, but hovering dream-like in invalid memory." So it's not surprising that she thought of the past with such yearning.

And yet the book isn't ruled by a mood of loss, or even the grimness that acquaintances sometimes attributed to her. Toklas's narration is funny, and often quite generous. Writing about the time she was conscripted into making dinner for a group because she was so clever, she quips, "It is certainly a mistake to allow for a reputation for cleverness to be born and spread by loving friends. It is so cheaply acquired and so dearly paid for."

In a chapter on slaughtering animals, titled "Murder in the Kitchen," she writes, "It was in the market of Palma de Mallorca that our French cook tried to teach me to murder by smothering. There is no reason why this crime should have been committed publicly or that I should have been expected to participate. Jeanne was just showing off." My favorite bit of Alice wit comes when she writes of approaching, with trepidation, the task of smothering some doves by herself for dinner: "A large cup of strong black coffee would help. This was before a lovely Brazilian told me that in her country a large cup of black coffee was always served before going to bed to ensure a good night's rest. Not yet having acquired this knowledge the black coffee made me lively and courageous."

In contrast to the *Cook Book*, Stein's books are not easy to read—not even the "accessible" *Autobiography of Alice B. Toklas*. I don't begrudge her this. I rather love the modernist project, which tries to evoke feeling and experience in the reader through form as much as content.

But I was delighted to discover that Toklas's cookbook is melodious and full of good humor, even as it casts a longing eye toward the past. As the journalist Janet Malcolm noted in her book on the pair, the *Cook Book* (perhaps unsurprisingly) omits the fact that for several years, Stein collaborated with the Vichy government, translating speeches for prime minister Philippe Pétain into English while hiding the pair's shared Jewish ancestry. Sidestepping this fact, Toklas instead filled her book with stories of making the best of a bad time. Several times, their home was conscripted by German soldiers, their household goods taken and consumed by the occupying force. But sometimes the soldiers were worth poking fun at. Toklas also writes about a humorous incident involving a German soldier who seemed to have heard that French butter was good but also didn't know what butter *was*. The man walked into a shop and ordered a full kilo of butter, and then things got weird:

The butter was weighed and wrapped up. Unwrapping one end of the package the German walked out of the shop. From the open door where I was standing I saw him bite off a piece of the butter. It evidently was not what he expected it to be for with a brusque movement he threw it violently over the garden wall of the house opposite. The story got about. People came to look at it. No one would touch it. There it stayed.

I've heard of people mistaking scoops of butter for ice cream and digging in with a spoon, but I can't even imagine what he expected French butter to taste like. Later she wrote, with more warmth, about a clandestine dinner with friends to celebrate her own birthday. An old friend acted as chef for the evening, using provisions procured on the black market, and it was a time of remembrance:

> After so long a fast we were pleased to indulge in more food than was perhaps going to be good for us. Someone remarked that fasts should be broken by a glass of orange or tomato juice. Eat, drink, and be merry, said I. Ah, if one were only certain in these days of dying from overeating. One remembered the packages of food one was sending to war and political prisoners and felt conscience-stricken at the overabundance of our feast.

That night, for all involved, joy mixed with melancholy.

But perhaps Toklas's most significant memory from her kitchen during occupation comes after German soldiers requisitioned their house and took various foods they'd saved to get them through the war. "In the afternoon, they left after helping themselves to our small supplies and souvenirs," Toklas writes.

"The jars of candied fruits were safely hidden in the linen closet. That meant a lot to me—they were a symbol of the happier days soon to come."

Toklas had candied the fruits herself over many months, along with jars of preserved produce gleaned from her garden and stored away for the lean, cold months. Discovering that the jars of sweet, crystalline fruits were still waiting in the linen closet was a harbinger of hope. Whatever else the war and the ravages of time might take from her, the promise of the future was still here, one in which eggs and cream would be available. There would be abundance once more. Those jars promised it.

IIIIIIIIIIIIIIIIIIIIIIIIIIIIIII

It didn't occur to me until I started writing this chapter to look up what the "B" in Alice B. Toklas stood for. To my delight, it stands for Babette, a name that makes me think of the cook in *Babette's Feast*, and the harmony between the two women is hard to ignore.

The tale of *Babette's Feast* first began as a short story by Isak Dinesen (a pen name of the writer Karen Blixen) and then was adapted into a 1987 Danish film directed by Gabriel Axel. The story is set in an ascetic religious community in Jutland, on Denmark's northern coast. Led by two aging sisters, this Protestant sect, founded by their father, eschews pleasure or joy that might come from any source beyond their strictly religious pursuits. It is into this community that Babette arrives, having recently fled a bloody political uprising in Paris during which her son and husband died. Though the sisters can't pay her, she works for fourteen years as their cook, making their severe and flavorless food. Then one day, Babette receives word that she has unexpectedly won the lottery. Her winnings: ten thousand francs.

The sisters are certain she will leave them, but Babette has another idea in mind. She asks the sisters for permission to cook a feast in honor of their father's centenary. The sisters are reticent at first—they'd planned to mark his birthday with only a simple supper for their small community, followed by coffee. But Babette prevails and orders ingredients from Paris.

If you've seen the film, then the next long sequence is likely among the most cherished of your cinematic culinary memories. Babette—who, it turns out, was a famous chef in Paris—spent every dime of her lottery fortune on the feast. Turtle soup. Endive salad. Blinis with fine champagne. "Quails in sarcophagi," small birds served in pastry shells. Rum cake, cheese, fruit, coffee, cognac, and an abundance of exquisite wine that first shocks and then delights the straitlaced parishioners.

At the end of the feast, Babette sits back, satisfied—she has done what she was meant to do. The grateful sisters are positive this is her last hurrah in their employ, but she amazes them by saying that she'll stay; she's spent her entire fortune on the feast. "Now you'll be poor for the rest of your life," one of the sisters exclaims.

"An artist is never poor," Babette says—having come to know, in the core of her being, what she learned from Papin, the Parisian opera singer who first told her to seek shelter with the sisters: "Throughout the world sounds one long cry of the artist: Give me the chance to do my very best."

In Toklas's cookbook I hear an echo of Babette's deepest longing: *Give me the chance to do my very best.* And what her book chronicles is a life lived not in the shadow of a genius, but quietly exhibiting a genius all its own—making, learning, exploring the way food creates in people something they didn't even know they needed. She begs us through her writing to treat cooking and food on its own terms: as an art form that can, and should, help us engage more fully with those around us.

Art is the thing we humans make that requires an audience to engage with it in order to bring it to its fullest expression. If you make a work of art, and nobody sees or experiences it, then is it really art? This is a question Toklas never had to consider, because food, by nature, is the art form that must be literally consumed by the audience. By many accounts, and quite unexpectedly, Toklas was not much for eating—she loved creating. But those around her ate, gathered, shouted, appreciated, and ultimately knew that there were two geniuses in the Stein-Toklas household.

And it turns out she was quite the writer, too. The final pages of *The Alice B. Toklas Cook Book* recount the pair's last days at their home in the French countryside. She extols the vibrance of her garden, the beautiful fruits and vegetables she grew, and the crates of produce she produced: "The cold sun would shine on the orange-colored carrots, the green, yellow and white pumpkins and squash, the purple egg plants and a few last red tomatoes. They made for me more poignant color than any post-Impressionist picture. Merely to look at them made all the rest of the year's pleasure insignificant."

I often think of this description while wandering the Union Square Greenmarket or enjoying my own patio garden's produce. Gardening is a marvelous artistic pursuit, as Toklas points out: "There was no question that, looking at the harvest as an economic question, it was disastrous, but from the point of view of the satisfaction which work and aesthetic confer, it was sublime." The careful attention to texture and color and taste and smell and feel was what mattered. What Toklas had learned from years spent cooking and eating in France was that growing food is as much an art as the one practiced later in their kitchens and at tables.

Toklas, by the way, never thought of herself as an artist. It's only in the final paragraph of her *Cook Book* that she vocally entertains the idea of being a writer. "Now it amuses me to remember that the only confidence I ever gave was given twice, in the upper garden, to two friends," she writes. "The first one gaily responded, How very amusing. The other asked with no little alarm, But, Alice, have you ever tried to write[?]" As if writing were harder than cooking well. But if you had friends like Toklas, it might be hard to imagine. Write? Like Gertrude? Like Fitzgerald or Hemingway or Eliot? Like the geniuses who had packed her apartment in the past, who had brought their wives and mistresses to the storied 27 rue de Fleurus?

"As if," Toklas wrote, affecting amusement—"As if a cookbook had anything to do with writing." But of course it did. Her words evoke rich, sensual experiences, informed by a life spent cooking for and feasting with those who made their art their life. But the real art, for Toklas, was in the living.

# F E A S T
## Brisk and Beautiful Gazpacho

I love that Toklas devotes an entire chapter of her book to cold vegetable soups. They're a weird sell for many people, especially Americans. But every year, right at the start of summer, when it starts getting very hot in New York City, I remember that they exist and that they're both the most delicious and the healthiest thing I could possibly be eating.

There are about a billion ways to make a fresh, cold vegetable soup, depending on your personal preferences and the ingredients available in your area. This one is mine, based on a recipe by Julia Moskin published in the *New York Times*. We can get tomatoes, peppers, and cucumbers in abundance in New York. Olive oil is always freely available. But I don't particularly like putting old bread in my soup, as called for in some gazpacho recipes. Mine resembles a smoothie more than anything else, I suppose.

So here is my favorite gazpacho recipe, the one I make all summer and leave in the refrigerator for an easy snack, where it gets more punchy as it ages.

---

2 lb. fresh tomatoes, cored and cut into chunks (everything is going into the blender). Plum tomatoes are really good for this, but big beefsteaks or virtually any other tomato will work just fine.

1 long green mild pepper, nothing too hot, seeded and cut into chunks. A bell pepper will also work just fine.

1 cucumber, peeled and cut into chunks

1 small mild onion—a Vidalia onion is ideal; a red onion will make it a little more pungent.

1 clove of garlic; normally I'm in favor of as much garlic as possible, but in this case I'd say go with just one, because the flavor increases in intensity as it ages.

2 T. sherry vinegar; you can also use balsamic vinegar for a sweet twist.

Salt

½ c. extra-virgin olive oil

---

1. Combine the vegetables in a blender and blend them till as smooth as possible, at least two minutes. You may need to pause and scrape the sides of the blender with a spatula to make sure everything is evenly blended.

2. With the blender running, pour the vinegar in through the hole in the lid. Next, pour in 2 teaspoons of salt, and then drizzle the olive oil in, too. The texture should go from chunky to smooth, and will likely turn bright pink. You want it to have a creamy texture.

3. You may want to press the mixture through a strainer to take out some of the solids, but I like my gazpacho thick, so to be honest, I never strain it.

4. Refrigerate the soup till it's cold.

5. Taste it every time you serve it, because sometimes the flavoring needs a little adjustment—more salt, usually—the longer it sits. Serve it in bowls, with olive oil swirled on top and some bread and cheese on the side. Make it art; make it worthy of attention and remembrance, whatever that means to you.

# More Salt with Alice B. Toklas

*The Alice B. Toklas Cook Book*: Alice's own book is delightful from beginning to end, full of great stories and memories. Plus good recipes, too!

*The Autobiography of Alice B. Toklas*, by Gertrude Stein: I recommend the edition that's been illustrated by Maira Kalman, for whimsy and to have an image to go with each tale. You get to see Gertrude and Alice's life through Alice's eyes, as written by Gertrude.

*Two Lives: Gertrude and Alice*, by Janet Malcolm: A short journalistic study of some of the odder and more unexpected points in the couple's life, including the nature of their collaboration with the Vichy government during World War II. Malcolm reflects, as is her wont, on the trouble of really knowing anything about people, which may be doubly true with Toklas and Stein.

*Charmed Circle: Gertrude Stein and Company*, by James R. Mellow: A comprehensive biography primarily focusing on Stein, but with plenty of room for Toklas, and a great way to get a feel for how truly far-reaching their social lives were.

CHAPTER NINE

# MAYA ANGELOU
## THE PERFORMANCE OF HOPE

When I started writing this book a
year ago and imagined myself con-
vening this dinner party as the
host, I pictured putting myself
at the head of the table. But
now, as I near the end,
I've come to realize an
obvious truth: Of all the
invited guests, the person
best suited to host would
have to be the writer, actor,
dancer, poet, filmmaker, public
intellectual, and legendary cook Maya
Angelou.

That Angelou was, on top of everything
else, a glorious, celebrated cook may come as a
surprise. It surprised me. Many Americans have
their first encounter with Angelou in school, where they're often
assigned her 1969 memoir *I Know Why the Caged Bird Sings*. In it
she depicts her childhood in Stamps, Arkansas, where she and her
beloved older brother, Bailey, were raised by their grandmother. The
book encapsulates, in direct and striking language, the experience of
growing up as a Black girl in the segregated South.

Angelou recounts fond family memories alongside harrowing stories of racism, trauma, and fear. Without sentimentality, she relates how she was raped at age eight by her mother's boyfriend. She told her older brother the name of the man, and four days later the man was murdered. Believing, with a child's innocence, that her words had killed him, she fell mute for five years, afraid to speak more. When she finally began to speak again, she knew the power of words afresh—and carried that knowledge into an adult life marked by a fierce attention to what writing and speaking could accomplish.

That conviction led Angelou through an expansive, almost unbelievable life. At sixteen, she became the first Black woman to be a cable-car conductor in San Francisco. She had her son at seventeen, three weeks after her high school graduation. She worked as a singer and a cook in a Cajun restaurant, a sex worker and a madam, an actress and an activist. She formed a dance duo with Alvin Ailey, who would later become arguably the most famous Black choreographer in history. She moved to New York to pursue a writing career, and then, after meeting Martin Luther King Jr., became the northern coordinator for his organization, the Southern Christian Leadership Conference. She moved to Africa—first Cairo, then Accra—and worked there as a writer, journalist, and university administrator. That's also where she met Malcolm X, who convinced her to move back to the US to help him build his new organization; shortly after she arrived, he was assassinated.

And that all happened before she turned forty. Her memoirs detail a long and incredible life, filled with friends like James Baldwin and Oprah Winfrey. She became the first Black woman to have her screenplay for a movie produced. She wrote and directed for TV and the stage; she appeared in the seminal TV series *Roots* and was nominated for a Tony for her performance in *Look Away*. She was also a professor—an impressive achievement given she never earned a bachelor's degree—and the recipient of many awards, including the Presidential Medal of Freedom. In 1993, she wrote and read her poem "On the Pulse of Morning" at Bill Clinton's presidential inauguration. The recording won the first of her three Grammys.

The list goes on and on. Reading any of Angelou's seven memoirs is like being at a dinner party listening to someone tell story after fascinating story late into the night, while crumb-covered dessert plates and empty whiskey glasses slowly pile up. The chapters are short, filled with tales in which Angelou is neither boastful nor bashful about her experiences and everything she'd accomplished. She saw the world, it seems, as a feast all its own—a place full of interesting people and things worth learning about and doing and fighting for. And writing about that feast was a way to share it with readers.

And yet, what she accomplished goes beyond mere productivity. She didn't simply add lines to her résumé and honorary titles to her name. Her work and life bore fruit. Anyone can produce, but only a healthy tree can grow something great to eat and provide shade for others to rest. And that, it turns out, is what Maya Angelou was always trying to do.

IIIIIIIIIIIIIIIIIIIIIIIIIIIIIIII

Fruitfulness is inscribed all over her life, and Angelou's memoirs attest to it. But the extent of her fruitfulness might be best observed in how she thought about food—cooking it, eating it, and sharing it with others.

In fact, Angelou didn't see much difference between writing and cooking. "I feel cooking is a natural extension to my autobiography," she told the *Guardian* in 2011. "In fiction, the story can be moulded to the author's needs but in autobiography you have to tell the truth. The reader has to believe what the writer is saying or else the book has failed. The same applies to cooking: if there is no integrity to the recipes, no one will trust them."

Telling the truth had been important to her since her time as an actress. While touring Europe with a production of the opera *Porgy and Bess*, Angelou committed to learning at minimum enough of the language of each country she visited to be conversational. She pulled it off, attributing part of her acuity to hard work and the rest to the capacity for memory and attention she'd developed during her five years of silence as a child.

It turned out that ability to learn and listen applied to her cooking, too. "I cook in different languages," she told an interviewer around the time her 2010 cookbook *Great Food, All Day Long: Cook Splendidly, Eat Smart* was released. "I wanted to offer to the reader a chance to actually be in Mexico or in Stockholm or in South America or in Mississippi. This book offers nice little visits to different parts of the world."

*Great Food, All Day Long* is Angelou's second cookbook, following her 2004 book *Hallelujah! The Welcome Table*. Both books are as much memoirs as cookbooks, though they're loaded with recipes. For instance, in *Hallelujah!*, Angelou writes of her grandmother who, as a young single mother with mouths to feed, started her own business baking and selling hot meat pies to local factory workers, eventually parlaying that business into a general store that would keep Angelou and her family well fed even during the Depression. She, of course, follows this with a recipe for "Fried Meat Pies," which are filled with pork and onions, turned golden brown in a pan full of shimmering oil.

In another chapter from *Hallelujah!*, Angelou recalls as a child being sent with her brother to the white part of Stamps to buy rare beef livers for dinner, and the long walk home, "back across the white zone I considered the frozen tundra," and then at last "wending through the black residential area where every house seemed to sing 'Welcome' and on to the store and Momma and the hot skillet." That memory is accompanied by a recipe for liver and onions. She writes about being a nineteen-year-old infatuated with a man and discovering he was two-timing her with someone else, so she went home and made herself a truly great banana pudding—recipe included, should we want to follow suit. There's a story about cooking a cassoulet for the renowned food writer M.F.K. Fisher, another about making pickled pig feet (also known as souse) with her fellow writer and dear friend Rosa Guy. She writes about making éclairs to fight writer's block, much to her husband's delight. Near the end, she makes smothered chicken for an up-and-coming young TV show host named Oprah Winfrey, who is delighted that Angelou remembers her name.

Each memory is tied to a meal, and that, to Angelou, is why making good meals matters. "If there is some event and at the same time the food you are eating is exquisite, then the food can help you to remember the incident, and the incident can help you remember the food you've eaten," she told journalist V. Sheree Williams in 2010. Writing about it is the natural next step, and good food writing is capable of creating magic: "When the writer tells the story, the memory of the food comes back so clearly that you can almost smell it cooking."

*Great Food, All Day Long* continues the story-and-a-recipe pattern, but from a slightly different angle. While Angelou's goal in *Great Food* is to offer some encouragement and motivation to readers looking to lose weight, she doesn't buy into "diet culture"—not at all. After her many travels, Angelou had become a wide-ranging eater, adventurous and thrilled by all kinds of cuisines, but the one thing she didn't have patience for was people who prescribed rules for eating.

In 1983, Angelou had a disastrous visit to a "health-food diner" with a heavily vegetarian menu. She ordered rice and greens— the preparation of which was bland and tasteless—and, to cap it all off, a waitress scolded her for her nasty habit of smoking. In an act of self-protection, she wrote a satirical poem that is very funny if you've spent much time in a particular kind of "nutritious" eatery, particularly back in the 1980s. "No sprouted wheat and soya shoots / And Brussels in a cake / Carrot straw and spinach raw, / (Today, I need a steak)," she declares at the start. Each stanza's refrain reminds the reader that she wants something savory instead—she is "dreaming of a roast," or "count[ing] on breaded veal," or craving "loins of pork and chicken thighs/ and standing rib, so prime." She eschews "seafood kelp" or "mushrooms creamed on toast," because "uncooked kale and bodies frail / Are sure to make me run." She prefers, she concludes, "any place that saves a space / for smoking carnivores."

You might conclude she just hates vegetables, but the poem is a cheeky bit of bluster. Like fellow Southern cook Edna Lewis, Angelou was a fan of the healthful foods she grew up with. Her cookbooks are full of delicious and nourishing food. But, writing in that era, she knew full well the tendency of the health-conscious crowd to draw lines around what was and was not okay to eat, particularly if you wanted to be "thinned by anxious zeal." Those kinds of rules—don't eat meat, don't eat butter, don't bread your veal, and for heaven's sake, don't have a cigarette or enjoy a glass of whiskey—simply did not fly with Angelou. The point of life was to *live* it, not just survive. Virtue doesn't come from what you eat or don't eat; it comes from how you live and love.

So in *Great Food, All Day Long*, her advice for the diet-conscious is this: "I have discovered that overeating can be countered by making the food savory and by eating small portions throughout the day and evening. The eater will be pleased with quality rather than quantity," she writes. You can't help but see that as a sly dig at a rules-obsessed diet culture. The recipes are nothing like what you'd find in a typical diet cookbook in the 1980s, maybe not even in today's paleo-fixated culture: rib steaks with parsley butter, eggplant parmesan, baked eggs with two kinds of cheese, mashed sweet potatoes with Grand Marnier, popovers made with real eggs, butter, and flour.

In one chapter, Angelou writes at length about her love of hot dogs and the rituals she's developed around their consumption, including raw onions, chili, and an ice-cold beer. When the hot dogs are ready, she says, they're her sole interest. "At that moment, I will not only not answer the telephone, I will not respond, even if my name is called by someone who knows me well," she writes.

So make really terrific food that's so rich and flavorful that you only want a little bit, and make it so good you won't let anyone interrupt you. And then you can have a little more later, when you're hungry again. It's not unlike today's notion of "intuitive eating," but you get the sense Angelou's been seeing life this way for a long time. In the chapter just before desserts (like crème caramel, or pears poached in port wine), she quotes Proverbs 25:16: "If you find honey, eat just enough." Then she follows with just two sentences of advice: "Whether speaking of honey or butter or ice cream, or anything, it is wise to eat just enough. You are going to be overjoyed when you manage your portions—even if just for two weeks." It's a gloriously simple philosophy of choosing joy over deprivation, and she concludes, as if to underline the point, with advice on how to serve great wine.

It's not surprising that she was committed to the importance of gathering and using only the freshest and highest-quality ingredients available. As she was fond of reminding interviewers, cooking and writing are really the same thing: "You need the best ingredients when you're going to cook," she told NPR's Don Gonyea in 2010. "The writer has to take some nouns, pronouns, verbs, adjectives, et cetera, and boil them up in such a way that you can throw them against the wall and they'll bounce." In the same way, she said, "when you cook, take these starches and proteins, and put all these things together in a way that the person who eats every day says, mm, this is really good."

Those who were lucky enough to dine with her discovered that for Angelou, cooking was not just about the result. After Angelou died in 2014, the historian Jessica B. Harris wrote in the *New York Times* about the meals she'd spent at Angelou's table in the 1980s and '90s: "Her larder was always prepared for a party, and she was the kind of cook who knew just how to put things together, effortlessly entertaining with stories and tall tales while the cooking went on." But what Harris remembered, more than the tastes and textures, was the process:

> What I do recall is the preparation. Her cooking was a virtuoso presentation that was part monologue, part dance routine, totally engaging and absolutely fascinating. There was a snippet of a song from a musical comedy at one point, a twist and a boogie at another and a flourish or two as a spice was added. It was a whole new form of dinner theater: a bravura performance calculated to astonish and delight. I was captivated, and from then on remained in her thrall.

Harris writes that she was not at all surprised when, years later, Angelou started writing cookbooks. They "replicated the astonishing performance I had seen decades earlier," she wrote. And they represented her "questioning curiosity" about culinary cultures from around the world.

The most important part of a meal to Angelou was not the food, but what the food fostered. "Food served is always more than just food served," she told NPR. "That is to say, it is more than just fuel for the body. Depending on who has prepared the food and who has served it and with what spirit, it can uplift." She adds that "around the world, in every culture, food is used to flirt, to be coy. . . . It can bring warring factions together."

Perhaps as part of her mission to pursue peace and justice, Angelou threw parties constantly, well into her later years, at her homes in both North Carolina and New York City. Everyone had to dress up. She used the best crystal and china she had on hand. (Her New Year's Day parties, held at her home in Harlem, were storied.) They were nights to remember and treasure.

That's why I think of her as a woman who was not only productive but who bore fruit. She worked immensely hard. She succeeded often, and failed sometimes too. But she also knew how to have a good time, and especially how to usher other people into that good time. A great feast can give a person a small taste of what it would be like to be in heaven. They are sheltered, for a time, from the storm, and given something that will nourish their soul as well as their body.

While being interviewed on stage by George Plimpton in New York, she expounded upon this idea:

> There is, I hope, a thesis in my work: we may encounter many defeats, but we must not be defeated. . . . In all my work, in the movies I write, the lyrics, the poetry, the prose, the essays, I am saying that we may encounter many defeats—maybe it's imperative that we encounter the defeats—but we are much stronger than we appear to be, and maybe much better than we allow ourselves to be. Human beings are more alike than unalike. There's no real mystique.

Every human being, every Jew, Christian, back-slider, Muslim, Shintoist, Zen Buddhist, atheist, agnostic, every human being wants a nice place to live, a good place for the children to go to school, healthy children, somebody to love, the courage, the unmitigated gall to accept love in return, someplace to party on Saturday or Sunday night, and someplace to perpetuate that God. There's no mystique. None. And if I'm right in my work, that's what my work says.

||||||||||||||||||||||||||||||

I hope it's obvious by now why I became convinced while reading her work that Angelou is the rightful host of this feast. Some quality of her work and life touches an aspect of every woman seated around our imagined table. Like Hannah Arendt, she believed in the radical power of friendship, of recognizing the difference of another from oneself and loving them all the same, and she was certain that recognition was rooted in the kind of social gatherings they both treasured. Like Laurie Colwin, she was convinced that the defeats we encounter and the mistakes we make, in the kitchen and otherwise, are a vital part of becoming a full person. Like Ella Baker, she worked fervently to uplift Black Americans and fostered relationships with all kinds of people around her dinner table, making space for the stories that lead to justice.

Angelou shared with Octavia Butler a strong commitment to the principle that power could corrupt, and that food can be a way to offer power, understanding, and equality to one another. Like Agnès Varda, she was joyously playful and very fond of leftovers. Angelou's food writing has a lot in common with Edna Lewis, not just in the types of Black Southern food they explore but in the way they join fond memories with hard ones, subtly challenging facile historical narratives. With Elizabeth David, she shares a delight in food from all over the world, and a desire to challenge her readers to try something new, to expand their palates, and to insist on freshness and quality. And like Alice B. Toklas, she believed in turning food into art, and saw feeding people as imperative to sustaining hope in hard times and in good.

Maya Angelou, I believe, would have appreciated being at the nexus of all of these fascinating, messy, beautiful lives and the stories they each had to tell. I can picture her in her Harlem brownstone, fixing up a feast, while Arendt clinks her martini glass against Baker's tumbler of bourbon, both listening and nodding along. Butler is browsing the vast library of cookbooks Angelou keeps in her kitchen, looking for inspiration, while Varda is peeling potatoes and foraging for the oddly shaped ones to set aside and photograph. Lewis is adding her Virginian flair to a few dishes; David is rummaging through bags of spices Angelou has collected on her travels; Colwin is offering her opinionated advice on the meal. And all the while, Toklas, quietly smiling, unpacks a bag with jars of her candied fruits, collected from where she'd hidden them away for a moment like this.

This scene is impossible, of course. But one like it is not beyond reach. Having spent the last year with these women, quietly sitting at their tables as they share their wisdom, I believe I have taken away a few lessons. Sometimes the lessons are simple; sometimes they're life-changing. The most powerful wisdom I met felt like common sense, but even that simple sense was radical, whether it spoke to politics, or to failure, or to friendship, or just to the importance of really good olive oil. I have reflected a lot on relationships between people, and how they are most often forged and bound together by sharing meals, and how hard those friendships can be to maintain when we can't gather over a meal. I have come face to face with my own desire to appear faultless and flawless, to not take up too much space, to avoid the risk of becoming too close to others or trust them too much. I have noticed in myself a failure to imagine the future by dreaming of what seems impossible. To believe in a better world to come.

What all of these women have taught me, in their beautiful, revolutionary lives, is the discipline of hope—to foster belief, and even confidence, in something that is yet to come. Angelou understood hope. She told Plimpton the root of that hope:

> I'm working trying to be a Christian, and that's serious business. It's like trying to be a good Jew, a good Muslim, a good Buddhist, a good Shintoist, a good Zoroastrian, a good friend, a good lover, a good mother, a good buddy: it's serious business. It's not something where you think, Oh, I've got it done. I did it all day, hot-diggity. The truth is, all day long you try to do it, try to be it, and then in the evening, if you're honest and have a little courage, you look at yourself and say, *Hmm. I only blew it eighty-six times. Not bad.* I'm trying to be a Christian, and the Bible helps me to remind myself what I'm about.

To me that's the definition of hope: to "only" blow it eighty-six times and still be able to say *not bad*, and then get up the next day and try again. It occurs to me now that one of the few things every human needs to do every day is eat and drink. And so, maybe hope is like eating and drinking: we have to seek it out, plan for it, celebrate it, and make sure it's nourished with the very best love and joy that we can muster, no matter what's happening in the world around us.

And we must share it, too. When I think of all we've experienced during the year I've been writing this book, and all we'll experience in the years ahead that I can't possibly foresee, I struggle to maintain hope. But I also know hope is something worth practicing. Hope makes each day go down as easy as a cold martini or a cup of gazpacho or a spicy shrimp salad or a big, hearty roast chicken shared among friends.

I wish we were having this conversation in real life. But I am grateful to have had this feast with you all the same. And I will let Maya Angelou give us a benediction, from that stage in New York decades ago:

> Most people don't grow up. It's too damn difficult. What happens is most people get older. That's the truth of it. They honor their credit cards, they find parking spaces, they marry, they have the nerve to have children, but they don't grow up. Not really. They get older. But to grow up costs the earth, the *earth*. It means you take responsibility for the time you take up, for the space you occupy. It's serious business. And you find out what it costs us to love and to lose, to dare and to fail. And maybe even more, to succeed. What it costs, in truth. Not superficial costs—anybody can have that—I mean in truth. That's what I write: What it really is like. I'm just telling a very simple story.

Feast by feast, friend by friend, nightcap by nightcap, hope by hope: let's grow up together, just telling our simple stories over a good meal, learning from those who've done it before us.

Thanks for coming, friend. Here's your coat. Don't forget your bag. I hope you enjoyed this feast and the company. And I hope to see you again.

Stay salty.

# FEAST
## POACHED PEARS IN PORT WINE

It seems only fitting to end with a dessert, and Angelou said many times that poached pears in port wine were her favorite. (She loved good wine, and also kept a bottle of sherry around when she was writing, to fortify her.) This recipe is more or less the same as the one in her book *Great Food, All Day Long*, though I've adjusted the measurements slightly to welcome in people who are more used to measuring by volume than weight.

Angelou recommends in her notes that any remaining servings get another chance tomorrow: "Seconds and third servings could be eaten in the morning with coffee or in the afternoon with a cup of aromatic tea," she writes. In other words, plan for leftovers so you can begin anew tomorrow.

---

4 pears

One 750 mL bottle (about 3 ¼ c.) of ruby port wine

2 c. water

¼ c. sugar

1 ½ oz. or 3 T. Cointreau (or another orange-flavored liqueur, or just orange juice in a pinch)

2 t. vanilla extract

Optional toppings: whipped cream, vanilla ice cream, mascarpone, caramel or chocolate sauce, or even yogurt

---

1. Peel the pears, leaving them whole. (You can use a vegetable peeler or a knife—just be careful.) Cut

off a thin slice on the bottom so that the pears can sit upright in the serving dish after they're poached. Leave the stem end intact.

2. In a large saucepan or other pot, bring the port, sugar, and water to a boil.

3. Put the pears into the liquid (you don't have to stand them up yet). Lower the heat and let them simmer, uncovered, for about 35 minutes. Rotate them occasionally so they poach evenly.

4. When they're done, lift out the pears with a slotted spoon and set them to the side.

5. Next, raise the heat and let the liquid in the saucepan boil vigorously for about 20 minutes, reducing the volume by half. The result will turn a bit syrupy.

6. Add the Cointreau and the vanilla extract to the syrup and stir to combine.

7. Place the pears upright in a serving dish, then spoon the syrup over them.

8. Place the dish in the refrigerator to chill for about 2 hours before serving. You can serve them with whipped cream, vanilla ice cream, or whatever else sounds good to you. And save the leftovers for tomorrow, a bit of hope for a new day.

# MORE SALT WITH MAYA ANGELOU

All seven of Angelou's memoirs are great, but start with *I Know Why the Caged Bird Sings*; if you can only pick one other, *Swingin' and Singin' and Gettin' Merry Like Christmas* is a bit of a romp.

*Hallelujah! The Welcome Table: A Lifetime of Memories with Recipes*: A truly fantastic little book, and accessible even if you don't know the first thing about Maya Angelou or aren't even really planning to cook anything—the stories are fun on their own.

*Great Food, All Day Long: Cook Splendidly, Eat Smart*: Angelou's second cookbook is no less delightful for technically being a "diet" cookbook. It's stuffed not just with stories, but with life. (And butter.)

*Wouldn't Take Nothing for My Journey Now*: Angelou collected her own short meditations and stories into a book for women. Full of wisdom and exuberance, there's something here for everyone. It's best read a nibble at a time.

# ACKNOWLEDGEMENTS

Writing a book is hard; writing a book during the worst, most locked-down phase of a pandemic is filled with its own special challenges, from finding a space to work in your small apartment to getting the books and research you need to maintaining enough concentration and sanity to actually write.

So I owe a tremendous debt to the people, places, and artists who helped me do just that. I'm grateful to Robert Clark, who one night years ago first gave me the seed of an idea ("Hannah's cocktail parties!") that grew into this book, and to Lauren Winner, Greg Wolfe, Paula Huston, and Tom de Zengotita, who taught me how to think and write good.

I'm so grateful to the people in my life who appear either explicitly or so obliquely they might not realize it throughout the book, most of whom taught me something about feasting and helped me through this time in one way or another: Tony, Carmen, Apryl, Luis, Trevor, Christy, Lee, Tyler, Laura, Chris, Sam, Caitlin, Mark, Katelyn, Roxy, Eric, Rachel, Erik, Vinson, Renee, Tara, Dhananjay, Isaac, Kyle, Scout, and the whole crowd from up the street, former, current, and auxiliary. And Mom, of course, who is the first salty woman I ever knew.

Many thanks to Adam for texting me salty language and ridiculous commiseration throughout this process, and also for mailing me the best wine I've ever had when I finished the draft.

Thanks to the bartenders of Swift, Mo's, Whiskey Trader, Camillo, and the White Horse, where I worked in spurts near the end of the book or outside on the sidewalk. I have learned a shocking amount about hospitality from you. Special mention to the bartender at Fiona's, where the bartender announced to the crowd the day I wrote the last word of my first draft that "she just finished a *book*!" and bought us all a round of drinks. And big thanks to the Airbnb hosts upstate who gave me space to think when the walls were closing in on me.

Thanks to Samantha Rose Hill, for teaching me (through courses at the Brooklyn Institute for Social Research) about Hannah Arendt. Huge thanks to my editor Lil Copan, who pursued me about the book and kept the faith through my various flailings and substitutions and tweaks.

Enormous thanks to Maya, Hannah, Laurie, Ella, Elizabeth, Edna, Alice, Octavia, and Agnes, for living well and, in your own distinct ways, being lights in the darkness.

Finally, my greatest, most inexpressible gratefulness to Tom, who not only gave me every single space and encouragement I could ever ask for, but made me martinis and playlists, excused my disappearances, cheered (literally) from other rooms, talked up the book to friends to an embarrassing degree, and pored over *three* drafts of the book, returning the most intricate and brilliant editorial suggestions I could ask for. I literally could not have done it without you. You are the saltiest, sweetest person I know. I love you.